Lasaine

THE LORD OF THE RINGS™

THE FELLOWSHIP OF THE RING

THE LORD OF THE RINGS™

The Art of
THE FELLOWSHIP OF THE RING

GARY RUSSELL

HarperCollins*Publishers*

HarperCollins*Publishers*
77-85 Fulham Palace Road
Hammersmith, London W6 8JB
www.tolkien.co.uk

Published by HarperCollins*Publishers* 2002
10 9 8 7 6 5 4 3 2 1

Edited by David Brawn & Chris Smith
Designer: Paul Vyse
Production: Arjen Jansen

A catalogue record for this book is available from the British Library.

ISBN 0 00 713563 7

Printed and bound in Singapore for Imago

Contents

THE FELLOWSHIP OF THE RING
Early concept painting
Alan Lee
"This is a painting I did for Peter, before anyone was actually cast, just to give an idea of the dynamic of the Fellowship and how they might look. So you've got Gollum fawning before Frodo, Gimli, Legolas, Gandalf and Aragorn, none of them of course looking entirely as they do in the actual film."

THE ONE RING
Elven lettering
Imery Watson
Above right is a conceptual design of the Elven lettering as it appears on the Ring. Imery took a live plate from the film and painted on the glowing runes using Photoshop.

Foreword

B y the time you read this, I imagine that you will have seen *The Fellowship of the Ring* film. Quite a few will have seen it more than once, many of you will have read the book, and some might even be wearing the inevitable T-shirt!

Although I had been privy to the odd snippet of film here and there while researching and compiling this book, actually seeing the finished film in December 2001 was the culmination of a nine-month odyssey into the world of Tolkien's Middle-earth – or, more accurately, Peter Jackson's Middle-earth, for he will be the first to point out that the film trilogy is just one interpretation of the Professor's book. For the people whose work appears in these pages, however, the film première was the culmination of a much longer period of work – for some of them, five years. That's a pretty long time to be working on just one movie project, albeit spread over three films.

I was very privileged earlier in the year to be able to go to Wellington, New Zealand, to visit the Three Foot Six studios (named in recognition of the average Hobbit's height) and see a lot of the work on *The Lord of the Rings* saga in preparation. The commitment, the dedication and the sheer love everyone had for the project was inspirational. Trying to bring that amazing feeling of energy to the printed page is pretty much impossible, for without their voices, their faces and their body language, the artists' pictures and words alone cannot tell the full story. However, I do think that the sheer quality of their hundreds of sketches and paintings –

some traditional, some using the latest digital techniques – give more than a hint of the literally awesome excitement and joy the designers had in bringing Tolkien's literary vision to spectacular life.

A few brief thanks – to Peter Jackson, who spared me what was supposed to be a brief amount of time but trebled it so we could talk about what was right and wrong with film-making today; to Fran Walsh and Phillipa Boyens, who appreciated that, as a non-Tolkien reader, I had no preconceptions about what things *should* look like (and appreciated more that I loved what they *did* look like); to Ngila Dickson, Randy Cook, Jim Rygiel, Barrie Osborne and Dan and Chrissie Hennah, all of whom welcomed me into their own worlds; to Alan Lee and John Howe, both of whom are far too unassuming and, I believe, don't realise how much they inspired everyone with their respect for the books as well as for their artwork; but most of all, to Paul Lasaine and Richard Taylor, without whom this book could not have happened.

I hope this book will show you that there is even more to *The Fellowship of the Ring* than you saw on screen. I just want them to get on and finish *The Two Towers* – I've seen the paintings already, and it's going to be fantastic…

Gary Russell
January 2002

Introduction

Although this is a celebration of the frequently unseen, often ignored aspects of film-making (from concept to execution) rather than a traditional behind-the-scenes publication – there are other books designed to do that – it is worth spending some time on introductions before "looking at the pictures". The best people to tell that story are those who told it to me – director Peter Jackson and the principal designers Grant Major, Paul Lasaine, Alan Lee and John Howe. But first, let's start with the production's chief wizard, Richard Taylor, head of the New Zealand effects house Weta Workshop:

"My partner Tania Rodger and I set up an effects workshop in Wellington 14 years ago. Over the years, we've moved around, eventually settling here about six years ago. I think we've got about 65,000 square feet of workshop space, which is pretty good. We operate five departments under the one roof, as well as Weta Digital, our digital

effects partner. On *The Lord of the Rings* we had 148 people in the workshop and 38 on set, operating over the five departments, in addition to the 200 artists at Weta Digital. There's a very small production staff in our workshop of six people who look after all of the day-to-day ins and outs of both the design, product development and production side and the on-set operation and post-production requirements.

"We started designing way back in the tail end of 1997. We've looked after the design fabrication and on-set operation of the special make-up effects and prosthetics, and the creature design and sculpting of the maquettes, including final-stage models used for scanning by our digital arm. Add to this the design, fabrication and operation of all the armour and weaponry, the building of all the miniature environments, from single towers to complex cities and landscapes, and we think it's the first time that one workshop has looked after so much on one film project. Some may think, 'Greedy!' but the fundamental reason that we put our hands up on the first day and said, 'Please let us look after so much,' is that we knew how important to the integrity of the work a single vision of Tolkien's world would be. It required a singular 'Tolkienesque' brush-stroke over as much of the work as possible. We felt incredibly passionate about trying to control the look as much as we possibly could from one place, so that the armour looked like it was worn by the creature who designed it that looked like it came from the land it grew up in.

"Weta isn't hugely experienced on the world stage, so five years ago it was an immensely ambitious thing to say we could do this. We have now reached the end of the project and are very proud of what everyone has done. We made the conscious decision to employ a number of young New Zealand designers, people who had never worked on feature films before, in order to bring a fresh perspective to the design, which I felt would best serve the old-fashioned innocence of the Tolkien's writing. We hunted out people who were passionate about the books and were also awesomely talented, creative people. We put together this team, backed them up with extensive research into appropriate periods of history, and with the much-heralded arrival of John Howe and Alan Lee, who lifted our skill-level immensely, we were then able to flesh out this huge and elaborate world and make something we could all be proud of."

Peter Jackson had been very keen for Alan Lee and John Howe to design the film – their award-winning artwork had adorned Tolkien's books inside and out in many countries throughout the 1990s and their work had come to be closely associated with *The Hobbit* and *The Lord of the Rings* by the millions who were reading them. However, Peter started by casting his net as widely as possible:

"We hunted out every piece of *The Lord of the Rings* art that we could find, because the advantage of *The Lord of the Rings*, as opposed to other film projects, is that it's been heavily illustrated before. There are all these calendars, books and paintings with different people's artwork, so we went on an intensive hunt to gather every picture that we could find that anyone had ever painted on the subject. That was when we learned about Alan Lee and John Howe. Those were the two who really inspired us the most.

"As soon as we looked at their pictures, we could see what the film should be like, where we should be heading. So we decided that it would be great to get Alan and John involved in the film if they wanted to. I had no idea whether they would have any interest in it or even approve of the idea of the film, because there are a lot of people who are heavily involved in the work of Tolkien who really didn't want a film to be made, and I didn't know whether Alan or John fell into that camp. So I contacted them, saying, 'Your paintings are inspiring us and we'd love you to be involved in the film.' Luckily for me, they were both more than keen…

"Alan Lee's artwork has a beauty and lyricism about it. His art captured what I hoped to capture with the film, which is a sort of graceful and gentle feeling… a poetry, I guess. Yes, he captured the poetic side of Tolkien incredibly well. John Howe is a master of capturing exciting moments. His artwork is almost like looking at a freeze-frame from the movie. He had already done a great painting of the waters coming down the river to wash away the Black Riders, and another of Sam fighting Shelob [to be seen in the third film]. His depictions of Gandalf were my favourites. His style is slightly less lyrical than Alan Lee's, but it represents a little bit more of what you would expect to actually film with a camera.

"So we had more of the poetic side with Alan, and the exciting, dynamic side with John. I certainly wasn't interested in rejecting all of their previous work and saying, 'Right boys, we're doing something original, this has all got to be new.' I was more interested in taking elements of what they had painted before that I really loved and extending it. So for people who have seen Alan's or John's artwork on the Tolkien books, there will be a lot of familiar things in the film. However, though I wasn't really into re-inventing for the sake of it, neither did they want to copy themselves, so they always took the previous pictures and expanded them and basically had a second go. I wanted

Title sequence ideas
Jeremy Bennett
These early ideas were put together by Jeremy Bennett after a series of brainstorming sessions between the various different strands of the art department and Peter Jackson. Jeremy's brief was to explore the credits for both the start and close of the movie, using the ring and, as discussions continued, gold and hot lava as the dominant motifs.

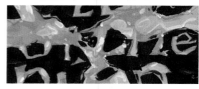

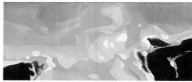

Title sequence ideas
Jeremy Bennett
Producer Barrie Osborne favoured this version of all Jeremy's concepts. He particularly liked the way the letters appeared slowly from the black, which becomes the crust of the lava. As the camera dives into the lava, the words are revealed.

them to be able to develop things that they liked and also change things that they didn't."

Having heard so much about the famous Alan Lee and John Howe from Peter, I thought I should ask them what it was like to work on the *Lord of the Rings* trilogy. Alan Lee takes up the story:

"I first read the book at a very young age, and it took over my life completely for a period. I didn't do many illustrations based on it until about 1990, when HarperCollins approached me about painting a celebratory edition of the work for the Tolkien centenary. There was a long period of discussion with Tolkien's family – I remember they were concerned in particular about how the hobbits were going to be depicted, so I did a couple of sketches, and they finally agreed to me illustrating the book. After that I got to do *The Hobbit* too, and so I became officially associated with the whole *oeuvre*. Despite that, I wouldn't say that I'm a huge fan – I'm not a person who reads it every year. It's obviously been an important part of my life for the past ten years, and I feel I know it pretty well now, but I don't actually know the book as well as some of the people at Weta, who are true aficionados. It's funny – people are terribly proprietorial about 'their' Tolkien, although because everyone here likes the centenary edition it has put a certain pressure on me to deliver the goods.

"I think my inspirations come mainly from reading the books, but also from having been thoroughly steeped from childhood in Norse mythology and other areas on which Tolkien himself had drawn. In some ways, there's only one way that I can draw Orcs and Goblins, and it's to do with my cultural background, stuff that's influenced me. So, to a certain extent, I just have to trust my intuition, priming it with the text, and having faith that the work that comes out will reflect what other people see in it.

"Working on the movie happened at the perfect time for me. I didn't have a contract for another book at that point, and I was ready for a change of scene. It's probably the first time in 20 years that I could actually physically leave Britain for an extended period without having editors screaming at me for deadlines!

"I'd always thought that *The Lord of the Rings* had fantastic potential as a live-action film – I was sure it was going to happen at some point. There had been discussions with somebody else about proposing a television adaptation, which was very interesting, telling the story over 12 episodes, but, like many other attempts, the ideas failed to materialize.

"Part of the attraction of this film was of course going to New Zealand. I've always been curious about the place; the few photographs I've ever seen of it greatly impressed me. And I suppose I had this idea of it as a kind of distant version of Britain, only cleaner, with taller mountains and weirder landscapes, almost like Middle-earth!

"When we got here, Weta had started doing some of the creatures. They'd done the Cave-Troll, they'd done a lot of work on the Orcs and various other creatures, but they hadn't done any of the places and the environments, and that became our job, really. Though we worked together on some of the designs, John Howe did more work on the creatures and armour, and Sauron and his fortresses, while I concentrated more on the places the Fellowship visit on their travels, like Rivendell and Moria. There were exceptions though, including some beautiful designs for Bag End and the Green Dragon.

"Peter Jackson would encourage us all the time to go that step or two further than we might normally have been inclined to, which had been basing our stuff just on what we knew from Tolkien's words. Peter's interest was in making the most interesting, exciting and dynamic visuals. Pretty soon we were into the game of extrapolation, the way Peter was thinking, so John Howe and I found ourselves trying to pre-empt what we thought Peter would like to see.

"I think our role, John and I, was to give form to Peter's ideas. He is very passionate about design, it's one of the most important aspects of the film-making process for him, so we tried to give him options and the breadth of ideas that he could then hone down and develop. He often had a quite clear idea of what he wanted to see, and we just fleshed it out into detail for him, but sometimes it was very vague, he only had a very loose idea of what he wanted to achieve, so we were there to give him options."

I caught up with John Howe in London while he was over promoting his book of Tolkien and fantasy art, *Myth & Magic*. I asked him how working on a film had been different to what he had been used to:

"When I first arrived in New Zealand, I was given the simplest brief – 'If you can draw it, we can do it!' Each time that a scene or an environment was in question, we'd sit down and run through the script, hear Peter's thoughts on it and then go and draw. Alan Lee and I arrived together, same day, same plane. We met for the first time at 30,000 feet over Singapore. We'd never met before although I wrote him a fan letter about six or seven years ago – he never replied! Then I got my courage up and phoned him and of course he was very polite and very nice. We got in touch with each other again when we knew we'd both been contacted for this project.

"There was never any question of territorial conflict of any kind between us – it went very smoothly because it turned out that the things that Alan does well appealed to him and the things that appealed to me were different, so as Alan was drawing Hobbiton I was working on Bag End or the Green Dragon. He moved on to Bree, I moved to other things. Alan knows England inside and out, of course, but I live in Switzerland so my vision of England is mixed with lots of continental influences. One day Alan and I were talking about style and Alan mentioned that the hobbit dwellings are very 'arts and crafts', and I said, 'What's that?' I had never heard the term, and realised I have these incredible holes in my knowledge of English culture. Then again, perhaps that helps when designing Tolkien's slightly fantastic world.

"When I started drawing for the film, I used a very big pencil, and drew pictures which were literally yards long and done rather quickly. My tendency was to do 15 quick pencil roughs rather than doing one or two with more detail. Eventually, thanks to Alan, I learned to slow down a lot and take a little more care and time – I wasn't used to doing sketches in my work and I don't have a pencil rendering style at all. I never do anything in black-and-white (or I never had until the movie), so the whole process was quite a new discipline for me, a real learning curve. I learned to put much more work into the actual rendering of the concept sketches so that there was something to look at rather than just a hasty, rough idea. I admire people like Christian Rivers, who does these incredibly detailed illustrations which give you exactly what you need to see.

"This was the first time I'd done a film project and it was a bit daunting at first. The whole process was to commit lots of ideas to paper and then refine them as Peter Jackson picked out the ones he liked. There was a curious atmosphere, because although we were aware that there was pressure to design so many things – it was a big project and lots of produc-

tion people were waiting on us – we never felt a noose around our necks at all, it was actually incredibly relaxed. I think the few times one of us missed a deadline, Peter would say, 'Well, you can't always time a creative undertaking. Sometimes it works and occasionally it doesn't.' This freedom actually encouraged us to work better. There was always a sense of expectation but no it-has-to-be-done-by-four-o'clock kind of pressure, which you get in lots of other fields.

"All of this (except the subject, of course) was so new to me – new industry, new continent, new hemisphere, new everything! Now I feel I'd like to do another film, but I'm a bit frightened that another project can't live up to my amazing New Zealand experience. I need to do two or three more movies to get an idea of what it's really like, because the whole *Lord of the Rings* experience was so extraordinary."

Paul Lassaine joined the design team once John Howe had left the film and principal photography was beginning. Paul was brought in to give a more finished look to the film, working on paintings that would represent not so much the design of places or artefacts but the colours, the scope and the actual look that the camera would see in the finished shots:

"I'd worked with Barrie Osborne, the producer, years ago on *Dick Tracy*. He called me and asked if I wanted to come on as a production illustrator doing concept paintings. The project I was on at Dreamworks was winding down, and I was going to be moving on to another project, which as it turned out got put on the shelf. So it was perfect timing, and I called back and said, 'Okay,' and we talked about me being in New Zealand for six to eight months. I was still there two years later with my own team around me!

"My role was purely as a visualiser. Peter Jackson doesn't do that. If he's not able to come up with a visual image of something he's got in his brain, he's got designers like us to help him. That's why he's got Alan Lee designing architecture, purely to put something down on paper so Peter can then start thinking about it in real terms. The art we do becomes something that can be used to show everybody else as well, almost like a trailer. Hopefully we were hired because we had a similar aesthetic vision to Peter's, so we follow him and translate his ideas to everyone else on the show. 'See this painting – that's what I want the Mines of Moria to look like,' and so on. Myself, Jeremy Bennett, Gus Hunter and the others are guides. We make

Title sequence ideas
Jeremy Bennett
A table-top setting for this concept, with the parchment and books being disturbed by a breeze. As the pages of the book are blown back, the title is revealed.

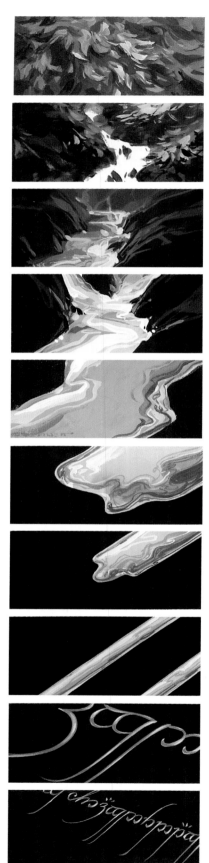

significant suggestions, create as many paintings as he wants, and he picks the ones he likes.

"Obviously the little pictures go fastest, because there's not so many brush strokes on them. Interestingly, though, it's not the size of the painting that matters, it's the thought that goes behind it and the planning. I can do a ten-foot version of a painting just by using bigger paintbrushes and still come out with exactly the same detail as a five-incher. Usually, I could do a couple of these a day, whereas one of the big ones, because there's so much detail, could take three days, maybe four at the outside.

"I often start with paint. Sometimes I'll have a little sketch first – I usually don't like to sketch that much and if I do, it's very minimal. The Lothlórien paintings, for example, didn't have any drawings at all, I just started painting. Actually, I started the first Lothlórien picture, the big Caras Galadhon one, and painted for about an afternoon before I stopped and just threw it away. It wasn't necessarily because I didn't like the painting but it just wasn't going in the right direction. That happens a lot, and rather than paint over or try and re-touch it, it's far better to start again. I generally work with a painting until I like it. Sometimes if I want something specific, I'll usually do a few little studies first before I go into it. I might make mistakes, little tiny things, but then I've got a pretty good guide for painting the big elaborate one. At that point it's just about added details – the painting doesn't really say any more to the director than the little one does, but people like to see the big ones.

"One of the ideas that we went with, and I was trying to keep this in my brain all the time – and I'm sure the guys designing the armour and props were really thinking in these terms too – was that the story is really like a journey back into time for Frodo and Sam. You look at the Shire, certainly Bag End, and it's almost like an old English farmhouse from the late 1800s, complete with furniture that you would find from that period – smoking jackets, pipes,

Title sequence ideas
Jeremy Bennett

Alan Lee actually storyboarded this idea, which Jeremy then developed and coloured up. It starts with the golden leaves, representing the opening of the story but these transform into darker, redder leaves and then lava, to suggest the transformation the story makes as it progresses toward Mordor. As this turns into molten gold, a variety of possible outcomes were devised. The one here sees it disolving into the same runic script that appears on the actual ring.

teapots, kettles, glassware, metalware, ceramics, all that is similar. Certainly Alan's designs reflect the Art Nouveau and have some Irish and Celtic influences. So you look at that and think England, maybe 150 years ago. It's pretty easy to place it. And as they go on their journey, every step they take, every new location they come to, is like going back in time a bit further. Aragorn is right out of King Arthur, as is Boromir, that puts you back in the 12th Century. Then they meet the Orcs, much further back, Mediaeval, Bronze Age, Iron Age stuff. The Dwarves, you picture them at a certain period, all the way back until you start getting into Mordor, which is like going into an almost primordial situation with cavemen. Finally, you go all the way back to Mount Doom, where the Ring was made and forged, which almost represents the creation. So it's a neat concept for a designer, it keeps you in line. I didn't come up with the timeline concept, but I was in on the discussion with Richard Taylor and the Weta guys. But who knows, maybe Tolkien had the concept in mind all the time."

To find out how everything came together design-wise, I asked Grant Major, the film's New Zealand Production Designer, to explain how all this work influences what finally appears on screen:

"Alan and John's art influenced everything, I have to say that. They started it all off because both of them came with this long history of illustrating the books. This is an English book, although the story is really more Euro-centric, so they lent a degree of European sensibility, which we could only imagine via the books. Alan and I, in particular, had a very compatible working relationship, and the look of the movie really grew from that.

"The story gets darker and darker and bigger and bigger as the Fellowship go further and further away from their respective homes, so it's quite like a road movie, where they experience new things and travel to another place and have more experiences. That was one of the major flavours of the movie, that they continued going into new lands, and we had to make it look authentic. From a budget point of view there had to be some re-using of sets, costumes and locations, albeit a limited amount, but the appearance of the film had to keep changing. Each society and each culture has its own look, and a lot of the developmental work we did was to establish those looks through architecture, costume, armour and props. Each society had to look homogeneous in itself but different from the last one. With Tolkien, there are a lot of histories involved as well. You can trace the cultures – they're often quite deep – so we needed to research all that, things like how the languages might appear engraved on their architecture or heraldry. There's a lot of really useful information in the other Tolkien books that helps flesh out the cultures. I had read *The Lord of the Rings* and *The Hobbit*, but went back and read *The Silmarillion* and *Unfinished Tales*. Also Humphrey Carpenter's excellent biography of Tolkien helped – by the end of all that reading, I felt I knew every nut and bolt of his world.

"We have used digital techniques to help increase the scale of the world on screen. I like to think that CGI is a tool, but it doesn't design things necessarily. It can be used for design, and it influences how much we need to build – there are a lot of set extensions and scenes can be a lot bigger, as they layer things up. The CG creatures are not going to appear on set, obviously, but there may or may not be a stand-in needed. In post-production they can colourise and recolourise things, and can go through the whole film to rack up the reds or the oranges or vice versa to enhance mood. I suppose this project is unique because of its size and the established history. A lot of that work happened after we finished the movie, so I didn't see a lot of the results until the movie came out."

Finally, while visiting Weta Workshop, I did notice there was more to designing than drawing and painting – there were shelves full of models of the creatures. I asked Richard Taylor how important these were to the design process:

"Our process basically started with discussions about the subject matter first, then research, then sketching, then colour illustration, of which we did a comprehensive amount, altogether a phenomenal body of work. Then from that, I'm a very big fan of three-dimensional maquettes, so we used those to finally capture an image that the director can see in 3D, that he can pick up and actually see in real terms. With some characters and objects, we only did a few, for others we did up to 70 different sculptures before we finally captured the essence of what everyone wanted. We tried to draw most of our design influences firstly from Tolkien's written word – as a rule of thumb, Weta's policy is always to go back to the written source if ever there isn't a consensus.

"For the look of everything, whether it's armour or pennants or general paraphernalia, our primary concern was to ensure that we drew from natural sources. We tried to stay within the palette of the ochres and the natural dyes of the area. To that degree, the first job that we had when we arrived on set, on any location, was to go and dig the soil. We would mix that with wallpaper paste in huge vats, and all of the actors and props were painted down with that particular ochre of the land. There were criticisms that the palette was very muted, but it was a conscious decision to try to make the Orcs look like they lived off the land and were part of the environment that they'd grown from.

"I believe strongly, and many people here agree, that the Fellowship and all the people they encounter are merely players on the surface of the film's most major character, which is Middle-earth, and that this is the story of the evolution of Middle-earth. Therefore, as often as possible, we were trying to make the characters feel as though they were elements of Middle-earth. That was very important to us, and I hope we succeeded."

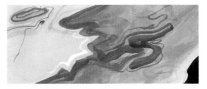

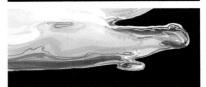

Title sequence ideas
Jeremy Bennett
Two more possible resolutions from the golden lava idea, one showing a map of Middle-earth, the other forming the title on a rich, black background.

Locations

Rivendell
Alan Lee
"This is an early conceptual illustration for the colour
scheme of Rivendell. It's just me getting my thoughts
together and I really like it. A little simple composition
for the colour study. All the colours come together."

HOBBITON

HOBBITON
Bag End
John Howe

"This painting was designed as a logo. I think I did this halfway through the project — Peter wanted a letterhead with calligraphy across the bottom of it. That's why the Black Rider is kind of cartoonish. He's not really like that in the film, of course. It's just to give some general idea of two central motifs in the movie."

▶ HOBBITON
Hobbit Holes
Alan Lee

"I did about 25 or so different Hobbit dwellings to go into specific spots in the location we had chosen for Hobbiton. Apart from their round doors and windows — and the fact they are half-buried underground — the houses have the look of English vernacular architecture from different periods, suggesting the area had been inhabited for several hundred years. I don't think any of us wanted to create startlingly new concepts for the look of Hobbiton. We wanted people who see the film to feel that they recognize it, that they really are in Middle-earth."

▲ **HOBBITON**

Bag End

John Howe

"These five above are all Bag End, except the second one, which is the doorway to the Green Dragon. These are just me toying with ideas for various doors and windows really, to give the designers some different options."

HOBBITON
Bag End
John Howe

"Peter wanted an idea of the perspectives inside Bag End — a notion of scale and how big a man would be compared to a hobbit. I didn't have the time to do a proper colour picture, so I used a lot of pencil and then put brushes over the top. I was really racing like mad — it was done in only a day. Mind you, I'm happy with the pot-hanger and that incredibly complicated column in the corner. The whole idea of shutters on the inside of these places is more European than English. I think of Bag End as the aristocratic residence, so it's much less humble than the other hobbit holes — and it seemed to me fairly logical that it should incorporate elements that are not purely indigenous to Hobbiton."

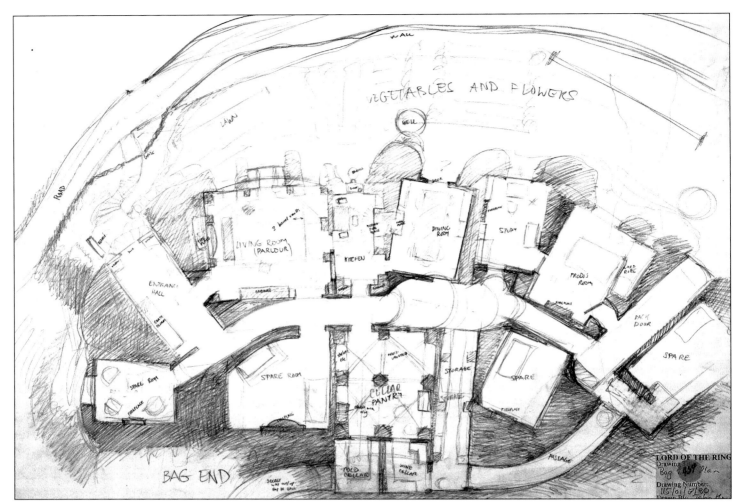

▲ HOBBITON
Bag End
John Howe

"The floor-plan was a pure extravagance on my part — totally useless! But, you see, I wondered where Bilbo's bathroom was! I mean, you never really visit bathrooms in films unless someone gets murdered or stabbed, and I was thinking, 'Well, where would it be, and how would it be set up, and where would the cellar be, and where would the sneaky Hobbity way out the back be, the secret passage to use in case you didn't want to go out the front door?' It was a lot of fun to actually design which rooms go where. Of course, in the end I didn't put the bathroom in! There was a problem with plumbing, because you really wonder what degree of sophistication Hobbits really have. Perhaps they just go round the back of the big tree!"

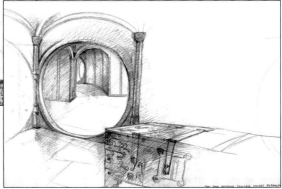

◄ HOBBITON
Bag End
John Howe

Going anti-clockwise, this is Bilbo's study. I wanted to make something cosy, with a writing desk and lots of treasures that he brought back — there's a Dwarven shield above the fireplace. Next is the entrance hallway — you can see this in more detail on the previous page, with the roots of the tree coming down into the back of the it. Below that is the fireplace in the living room. I'm totally enamoured of the huge ceramic stoves that people used to have, two or three yards tall, and covered in very ornate decorative tiles, and I thought Bilbo might have a Hobbit version of one of these. At the bottom of the page is Bilbo's wine cellar, followed by his bedroom and finally the dining room where, as Lord of the Manor, he's always prepared for lots of guests."

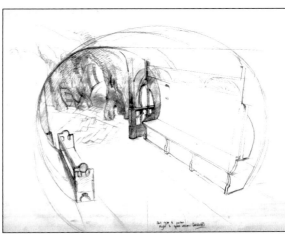

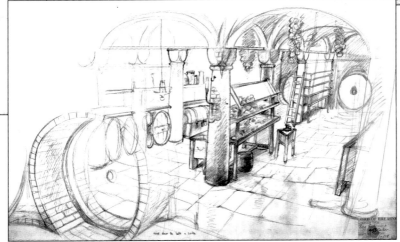

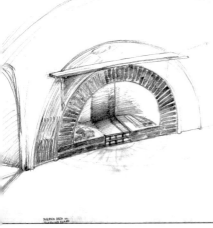

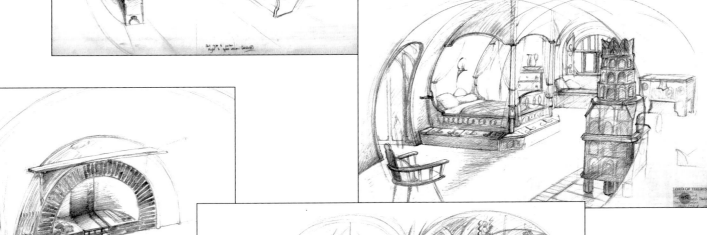

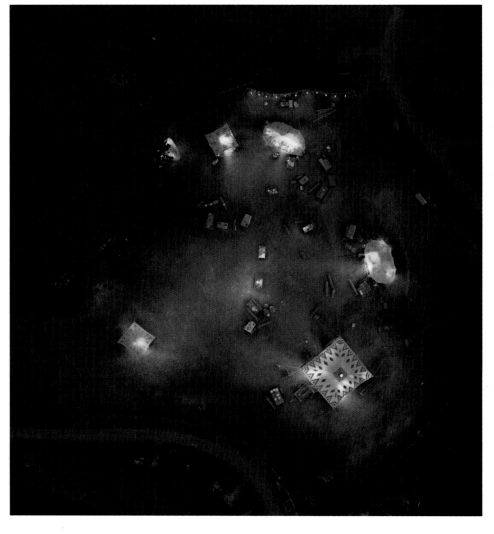

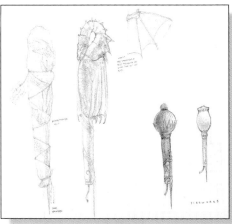

HOBBITON
Fireworks
John Howe
The sketch above shows some early designs for Gandalf's fireworks, including the Smaug one, released prematurely by Merry and Pippin to spectacular effect.

HOBBITON
The party field
Yanick Dusseault
This painting was created as a backdrop for the Smaug firework as it shoots upwards into the sky and towards the camera.

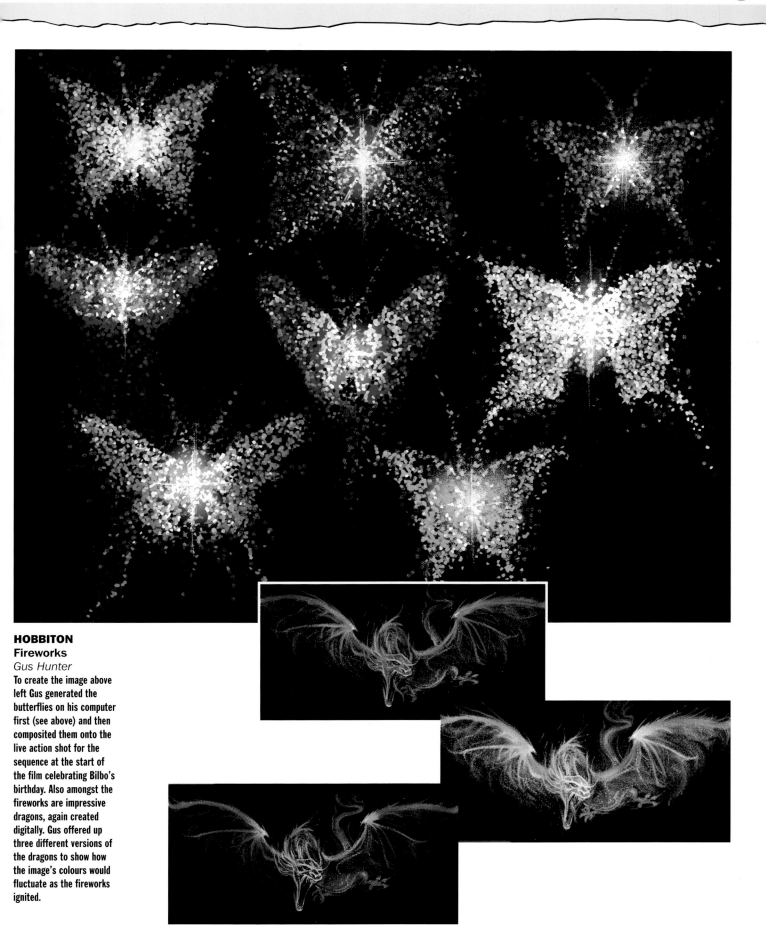

HOBBITON
Fireworks
Gus Hunter
To create the image above left Gus generated the butterflies on his computer first (see above) and then composited them onto the live action shot for the sequence at the start of the film celebrating Bilbo's birthday. Also amongst the fireworks are impressive dragons, again created digitally. Gus offered up three different versions of the dragons to show how the image's colours would fluctuate as the fireworks ignited.

◄ **HOBBITON**
Fireworks
Gus Hunter
These were some conceptual ideas showing the colour, style and scale of the firework spears. The shots also demonstrate the flow of movement as the fireworks move through the night sky.

▲ **HOBBITON**
Smoke rings
Gus Hunter
These two shots from shortly before Bilbo's party demonstrate the intricate patterns capable of being created via CGI. The ship itself was taken from a design by Alan Lee, because Peter Jackson thought a ship was more dramatic than the traditional boats seen elsewhere in the film.

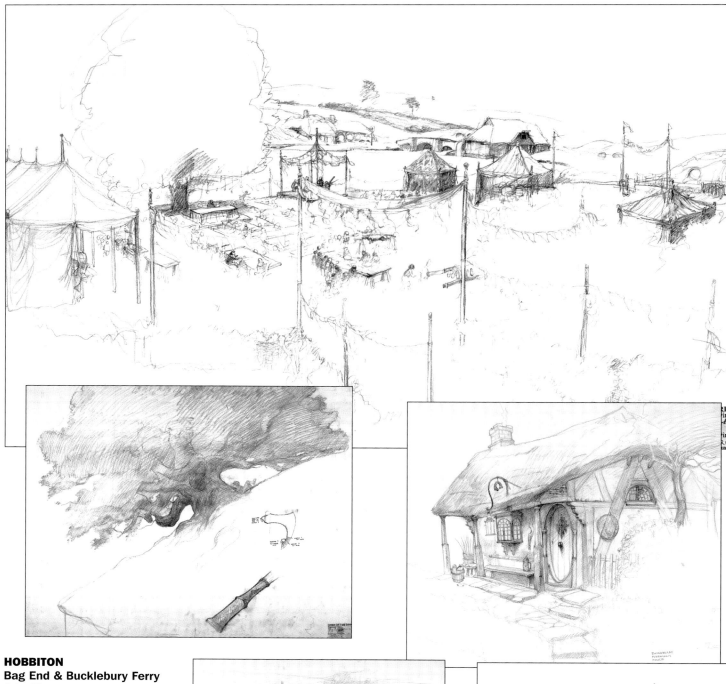

HOBBITON
Bag End & Bucklebury Ferry
John Howe

"Going clockwise, this is the tree above Bag End. I think I was just doodling that one, it was just one of those moments when I was doodling lots of different things — thinking of this tree — and an axe head or something. Next is the Ferrymaster's cottage, which was to be situated just up the hill from the ferry, which the Hobbits use to escape the pursuing Ringwraiths."

◀ HOBBITON
The party field
Alan Lee

"This is the basic idea for the big party field with tent poles for bunting and bouquets to be put on. The sort of thing to keep Dan Hennah happy. While I was based in the studio, he was out on location, as Art Director, making sure it all looked good. He'd keep an eye on the way it was developing and make sure it was in keeping with everything else."

▶ HOBBITON
The Green Dragon
John Howe

"The Green Dragon is a Hobbit pub. I've never seen a real country pub. We don't have them in Switzerland. The Green Dragon was intended to be a rambling one, which would be a Hobbit hole that had been built up from a bank into an actual building and become an inn, a meeting place. It's really the only place they socialize in great numbers.

The idea was to have a market square out front. When these pictures were drawn, I believe we had already chosen the location, because I added that water down in the front. In the finished film they just stay outside — but at one point, Peter Jackson was toying with the idea of having scenes inside, looking out through those windows, so I sketched those interiors. The other exterior picture shows the stables next door. Beneath this is a selection of Hobbit farming implements."

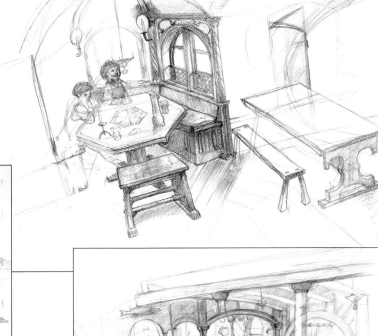

BREE
Town Square
Paul Lasaine

"This is adapted from one of Alan Lee's earliest sketches. It was painted before they shot the live action, and it's pretty close to the final thing. Actually, this is a little brighter than I would have liked, it's supposed to be under dense cloud, and it is raining. The rain will be added digitally. This kind of painting is done mainly as a rough guide for the matte major of the shot, but also as a colour guide for the mood."

BREE
Entry Route
Roger Kupelian with Mark Sullivan

In this matte shot, the two artists took the shot as filmed on location (top) and then added the matte background (below). Amongst the changes are the new roof on the foreground left building and the scaling down of the foreground right barn. The film crew's trucks and generators have been replaced by the houses and inns of Bree itself.

BREE
Town Square
Alan Lee

"These are some early concepts for Bree. I was trying to get to grips with the architecture, trying to bring in the ramshackle and aged and twisted look. The top one is closer to what we actually ended up with. It's basically a medieval English city-look: some of the buildings were drawn from photographs I'd taken of buildings in Exeter from around the fifteenth and sixteenth century. All that nice timber and thin walkways. Exeter is really beautiful and lent itself to Bree perfectly."

BREE
The Prancing Pony
John Howe

"The version of the Prancing Pony above was very grandiose but ended up being much humbler in the film. I wanted to make it as intimidating as possible, absolutely huge, but I'm not quite sure that my version exactly fits the mood. To the right are the courtyard and stables. And yes, that is a little Watcher doodle which seems to have come floating in!"

BREE
The Prancing Pony
Alan Lee

"The interior of The Prancing Pony is based on a number of pubs that I am familiar with, where I live. I'm not a great pub-goer but a country pub is always very pretty and Devon is full of the best ones. We decided that at The Prancing Pony, as you come in through the main doorway, the bar would be to the left and there is a kind of reception area where the Fellowship ask for directions."

LORD OF THE RINGS
Drawing Title:
Prancing-Po 249

▲ **WEATHERTOP**
Wide shot
Gus Hunter
Working from some of Jeremy Bennett's concept sketches, based on the actual footage shot on location, Gus engineered this dramatic view by adding various background layers and sky elements in Photoshop.

WEATHERTOP
The architecture
Alan Lee

"The statues on the opposite page are from the area around Weathertop — because Weathertop is one of the seats of the Palantír, I thought it would be nice if all these statues were carrying stone balls. These other two drawings are alternate day and night looks for the place."

WEATHERTOP
The Approach
Max Dennison
A before (above) and after (below) shot of Aragorn leading the Hobbits towards Weathertop, the film's first view of the ancient ruins. The actual structure atop the mound is a matte painting which has been digitally composited into the live-action sequence.

WEATHERTOP
The Approach
Max Dennison

The top image is a view of Weathertop at dusk — a shot in which Aragorn walks out onto a small ledge and is silhouetted against the sky. Because the original shot was filmed during the daytime, all aspects of the lighting for this necessitated major changes. The lighting changes were altered even further for the lower shot of Weathertop at night. Everything Aragorn can see — the fire that the Hobbits have lit, the mist, the sky and, of course, the ruins — are all matte paintings.

ISENGARD

◄ **ISENGARD**
The Approach
Alan Lee
"This is quite a straightforward piece, which I used to show not only the look of the walls, but to give some sense of the size of them"

ISENGARD
Gandalf's Approach
Paul Lasaine

"This is the first time we see Isengard in the movie. Basically, what you have in this composite is the live action that was shot which in this case is Gandalf riding. That's it. Everything else is a composite of about six or seven different photographs — none of what you see here was actually there bar the man and horse. We knew we wanted this particular valley as the Isengard valley, so we went down to the South Island and shot it. The base of the mountain on the left was nearby, but not the same valley. The rear mountains are two or three other ranges, and then there are the trees to the right. We knew we wanted the look of Gandalf riding down and seeing the ring of Isengard out there, which would have been behind those trees. So we actually changed the perspective on the shot completely, made it look like something new. None of this is on a hill here, but we made it look like it is. As always with good visual effects, you're not supposed to know that none of the area other than the ground the horse is on wasn't actually there. So while the guy watching the film is going 'Wow, I know there's no tower there, but how've they done that?' they're not realising that none of it was there. That's when it's really cool, when no one has any idea how much of the scene is artificial. It's a classic matte painting thing to do — where the location doesn't exist, you make it up.

It's the same thing with the shot of Gandalf riding under the archway — a mixture of miniatures and mattes. The dip outside the arch is fake, as are the holes in the wall itself — the shadows cast from trees that aren't actually there. But hopefully you can't actually tell in the finished sequence what is and what isn't real."

LORD
Drawing
Iseng
Drawin

ISENGARD
The Caverns
Alan Lee

"These are drawings for the Isengard Caverns, where Orcs are working to arm and equip an army of Uruk-hai, who have been specially created to serve Saruman. This area is briefly alluded to in the books, but Peter and Richard saw the potential for creating some stunning and dramatic set pieces. Both John and I did drawings of the pits and machinery and I made a maquette of the caverns which served as a starting point for the miniature.

"The size and complexity of the miniature grew as Peter started to work out what he wanted to do with it, and I'm still trying to work out how Alex Funke filmed some of those awe-inspiring shots."

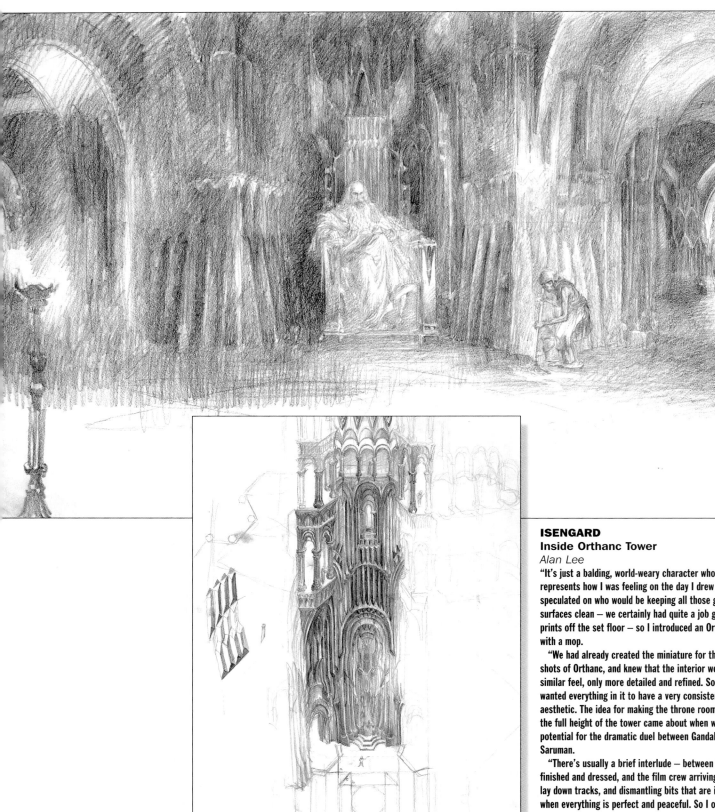

LORD OF
Drawing Title
Ort
344
Drawing
155/01/
Drawn By:

ISENGARD
Inside Orthanc Tower
Alan Lee

"It's just a balding, world-weary character who probably represents how I was feeling on the day I drew him. I also speculated on who would be keeping all those glittering surfaces clean — we certainly had quite a job getting footprints off the set floor — so I introduced an Orcish cleaner with a mop.

"We had already created the miniature for the exterior shots of Orthanc, and knew that the interior would have a similar feel, only more detailed and refined. So we wanted everything in it to have a very consistent design aesthetic. The idea for making the throne room extend to the full height of the tower came about when we realized the potential for the dramatic duel between Gandalf and Saruman.

"There's usually a brief interlude — between the set being finished and dressed, and the film crew arriving, starting to lay down tracks, and dismantling bits that are in the way — when everything is perfect and peaceful. So I often took advantage of this to sit, and inhabit the space, the opportunity of stepping into one of your own drawings being too good to miss."

ISENGARD
Inside Orthanc Tower
Alan Lee

"These two drawings are getting quite close to the look of the finished set. It was built up to about seven metres and the rest of the interior was modelled digitally. The drawing below also shows the lamps that were made by Natalie Staniforth, a talented sculptor who came out from England to work on the project.

"There are some other things going on in that drawing, too: and Elf, some doodles, and Gandalf's staff. Someone may have just reminded me that we needed three different staffs for Gandalf. He loses his first one in Orthanc and the second in Moria. We looked for some pieces of wood that had the right knotted-root look, but then I drew something and it was sculpted by Brigitte Wuest — another brilliant sculptor."

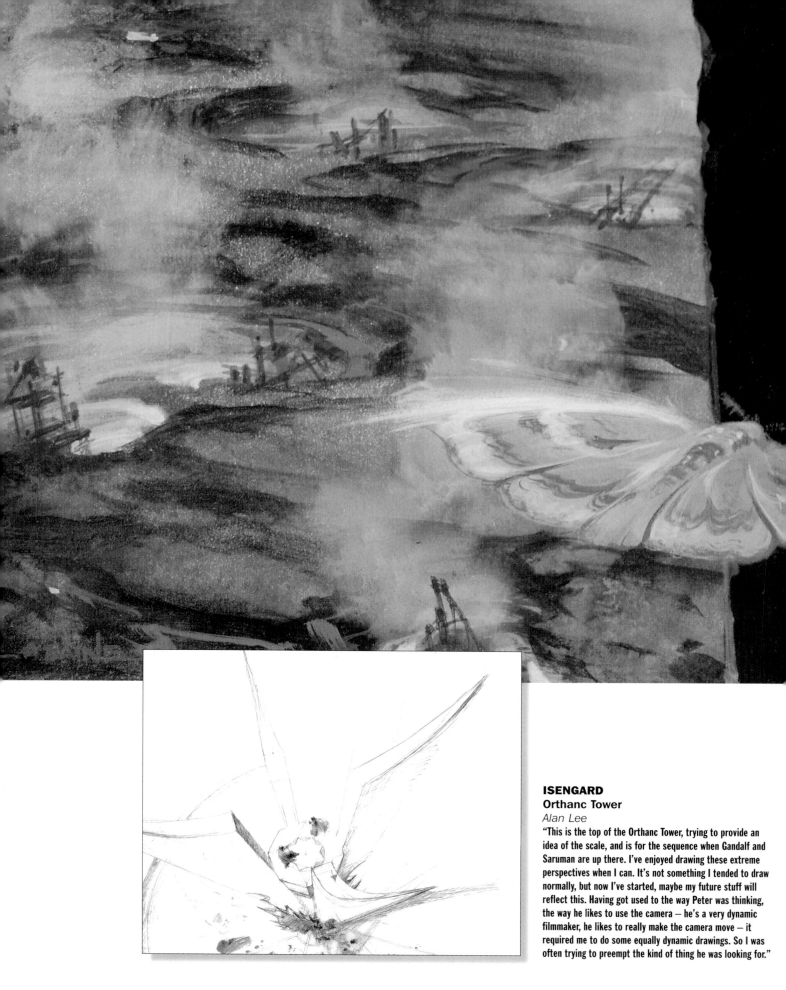

ISENGARD
Orthanc Tower
Alan Lee

"This is the top of the Orthanc Tower, trying to provide an idea of the scale, and is for the sequence when Gandalf and Saruman are up there. I've enjoyed drawing these extreme perspectives when I can. It's not something I tended to draw normally, but now I've started, maybe my future stuff will reflect this. Having got used to the way Peter was thinking, the way he likes to use the camera — he's a very dynamic filmmaker, he likes to really make the camera move — it required me to do some equally dynamic drawings. So I was often trying to preempt the kind of thing he was looking for."

ISENGARD ▲
Orthanc Tower
Paul Lasaine

"This one, the Moth Shot I call it, was done after a request from Peter Jackson. Primarily it was to show the first time that we actually see Isengard as a destroyed, wasted Isengard. Up until then, it was this beautiful forest garden. We follow this moth in a crane up over the wall, and there it is, essentially a big industrial wasteland. This was a colour-study, really, done sometime before anything was actually shot. We were interested in the development of the valley. The crew actually had this with them when they filmed the location shots and so when it was time to do the final matte work, it would be exactly as Peter had intended way back when we started on this painting."

◄ **ISENGARD**
Gandalf's Rescue
Paul Lasaine
This early colour scheme was to give an idea of scale for the digital artists to compare Gandalf against Gwaihir, and also to show how they would be lit in the moonlight.

ISENGARD
The Caverns
Jeremy Bennett

The painting of the Uruk-hai below Isengard (left) was the
result of about 50 sketches and compositions created to
resolve foreground, background and midground elements of
the final shot. The scale of the Uruk-hai and the caverns was
of some concern, thus this painting was needed to set the
perspectives. The rough pencil version (above) was actually
used by Alex Funke, the Director of Photography, for the
miniature set-ups. He taped Jeremy's sketch onto the
monitor on the miniature stage and lined up his shot against
the pencils, which was very satisfying to the artist — a rare
chance for the artwork to be used so literally.

▲ **RIVENDELL**
The Ford of Bruinen
Gus Hunter

The above two composites, created in Photoshop by Gus, were the first illustrations of how this spectacular scene would look in the film. They show the water-based horses — summoned by Arwen — in relation to their environment, and to the Ringwraiths and their horses prior to the deluge that washes them away. The image of Arwen on Asfaloth can be seen in the top image.

RIVENDELL
Colour schemes
Jeremy Bennett

After Alan Lee and Paul Lasaine had done their basic design concept work for Rivendell and its environs, the miniature was built by Weta. Jeremy then painted these colour schemes prior to the film unit going out and shooting any footage to suggest how the miniature might look ideally in the finished film, when the various natural light and digitally enhanced light sources are present.

RIVENDELL
Balcony Sequence
Jeremy Bennett
"These are two passes at the same shot. The lower one came first, the top one was more to Peter Jackson's preference. This is a take on a painting of Alan Lee's, I think it's from the Lord of the Rings book he illustrated. I just added more of a romantic colour scheme to it. He did it in yellows and greens, and I was actually going for a more rustic feel. So we went from there to here to get a different concept, a different framing on it. There's so many little influences — the whole kind of Prague architecture, there's a lot of Art Nouveau, some Italianate and other stuff, mingling with Celtic design. Alan designed all that."

RIVENDELL ▶
Balcony Sequence
Paul Lasaine
"This is a Photoshop composite of the finished sequence — it uses the live action shot of Elijah, with a miniature in the midground and then matte paintings for the backgrounds. The trees and things on the cliffs came from various sources."

RIVENDELL
Colour schemes
Jeremy Bennett

After completing the colour studies (see previous spread),
Jeremy started to lay out the actual Rivendell valley.
Although a number of possibilities were drawn, this was the
one that Peter Jackson liked the most, and it set the tone
for the rest of the Rivendell sequences.

RIVENDELL
Living statues
Alan Lee

"These were ideas for the living statues that surround
Rivendell, carved from trees which had then gone on
sprouting, adding to the majesty and uniqueness of each
one. And passing beneath them is an Elven rider, just for
scale. It's the same thing with the living archway, but we
didn't go with that in the end. It's just one of the hundreds
of things we designed that there wasn't enough time or
perhaps the need to create. But I do like the way they
suggest Rivendell's ease and peace with nature."

RIVENDELL
The Fellowship departs
Gus Hunter

Two matte painting composites which when combined form
the finished frame (with the painted figures to be replaced
later with the actors). These utilize miniatures in the
foreground and digital mattes for the backgrounds such as
the waterfalls and the mountainside. The sunlight, to suggest
the bright morning, is similarly generated on the computer.

RIVENDELL
Various design sketches
Alan Lee

"The top illustration is a drawing that was done specifically for the model makers to show the foundations of Rivendell so that they could build all the rock work, and thus the buildings that would be sitting on top. I left them out because, quite simply, they'd be in the way and the people at Weta wouldn't get a real idea of what the base should look like. The picture below is just an idea I had for the structures of Rivendell, this time utilising a tower, and it's not too dissimilar to some of the buildings we ended up with. They veer towards a cross between a Japanese temple and Frank Lloyd Wright. The idea of the building nestling amongst the trees, co-existing with nature, really appealed to me, all these trees being very organic within the stony surroundings. At the bottom of the page is the painting for Elrond's Chamber. It's not the final design, indeed it's a very early one. It shows the battle between Isildur and Sauron. It doesn't happen like this in the movie so, as I painted the actual prop in the film, I was able to change it easily, to match what Peter shot."

RIVENDELL
Various sketches
Alan Lee

"This picture above is the library, a very early idea. We ended up incorporating a number of the elements from this into what eventually became Elrond's Chamber. The library might have been one of the first things we drew, and that gave us all the ideas for the other sets around it. You can see the trees outside growing inwards, adding to the atmosphere. The library exterior is the picture on the right, whilst below is an idea for Elrond's Chamber prior to the adaptation of the library designs."

RIVENDELL
Various sketches
Alan Lee

"This one at the top is a concept for the look of the Rivendell architecture, and demonstrates the way the cut-out areas in the buildings would accommodate movement for the trees, as in the library, so that you get the impression the place was built around nature rather than into it. Rather than hanging pictures in their bedrooms, they'd have windows that allowed real nature to enter and form some sort of central image. It's a kind of indoor/outdoor idea that is again a reflection of the ideal place I'd like to live in. The picture on the right is a quick design sketch of the Pavilion in Rivendell, which was going to be made on location, so it needed to be easily moved, quite lightweight. At the bottom is another view of the library exterior, showing a reverse of the way the trees grow in and around the buildings."

RIVENDELL
Exterior composite
Paul Lasaine, Gus Hunter & Wayne Haag

"There are a number of elements here. You see, apart from everything else, I've been actually involved in directing the scenic unit. What we did was go out and hire a brilliant New Zealand photographer, Craig Cotton, and he became our Director of Photography for the scenic unit, but doing stills. There's a little bit of moving stuff as well, but primarily we were doing stills work, shooting these big panoramic environments that can then be scanned into a computer and turned into digital backgrounds for anything. We used these as augmentations instead of what would have been matte paintings in the old days, or someone actually painting them onto glass.

"So with Gus on the computer, we used these photographic elements plugged directly in. We did thousands and thousands of photographs all around both North and South islands. With this shot of Rivendell we went to a location that looked like what might become the cliffs, and shot all different angles, a whole panorama, 360 degrees — we did a lot of work from helicopters as most of the big shots required that big aerial look. We then came home and piled them all together. These then become super high resolution images that we could zoom right in on, and use for multiple scenes. A lot of what we did with Rivendell was to use those compiled elements, and if there was something missing, well, it was either use a photograph that we'd scanned out of a book or something that we'd scanned from somewhere else. So Rivendell for instance has this river in it, from the northern part of the South Island, and this mountain is from somewhere else entirely and so on. Very little of the original mountain we shot still exists here bar the basic landscape outline. Then we added in the actual Rivendell miniature, a lot of painting and more stills from around New Zealand. All these waterfalls are actual, real waterfalls from both New Zealand and elsewhere that we'll move digitally. They're made up from bits of hundreds of waterfalls. They then have a mist effect added.

"Gus did another version of the scene above. This shot is basically when the Hobbits enter Rivendell, late afternoon when it's lit like this. But when they leave, it's a different time of day, so what Gus did was take the light, flipped it, so it came from the other side, basically turning this into a morning shot. It's actually painted, but digitally painted. Within Photoshop you have things like colour controls, so you can screw around with colours and lighting all you want."

◀ **RIVENDELL**
Colour scheme
Paul Lasaine
Before work began on the digital composites, Paul painted this colour scheme for Peter. This gave him an idea of how light would fall on the Elven refuge, situated as it was in a steep-sided valley. Paul based this picture on the Alan Lee painting that appears in the illustrated edition of The Lord of the Rings.

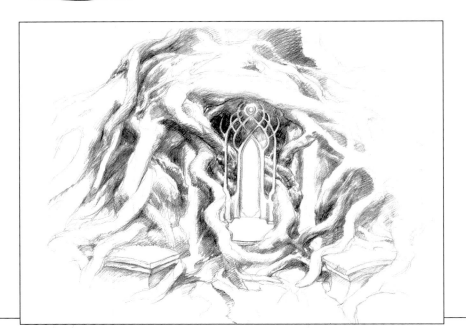

RIVENDELL
Elrond's Chamber
Alan Lee

"This was an idea for Elrond's throne which incorporated these tree roots, giving it a very rough and earthy feel. It's sitting amidst the tree rather than actually carved out of it and I quite like this, but in the end the final setting was a little less intricate, less complicated I think. Below that is an early rough of the Council Chamber which changed considerably once we sorted the environment out. At this stage we were designing a specific building for the Council Chamber but in the end it was felt that the Council Chamber and Elrond's Chamber would be too expensive to do separately so we combined elements of all our ideas, including those of the library, into one final set. The statue, bottom left of the page, was a device for creating a nice symbolic image, to add to the sense of importance in which Narsil is held. Next to that is a sketch of Galadriel when she undergoes a bit of a change! The statues to the right of that are just other ideas, nothing too intricate."

RIVENDELL
Elrond's Chamber
Alan Lee

"Above and below are roughs for Elrond's Chamber so that the plasterers and builders could have some very specific and detailed ideas to work from. To the right is the Council Chamber once again, with a bird motif. They turn up quite a lot in Rivendell, something I often added in — I tended to add swans and things to some of my original Tolkien paintings — birds seem appropriate for Elven symbolism."

RIVENDELL
Various sketches
Alan Lee

"It's that statue again, holding a shield and looking mournfully down at the broken Narsil. It's hidden away, nestling in the hollow of a tree, again suggesting the mix of the two natural elements, stone and wood."

THE MISTY MOUNTAINS

THE MISTY MOUNTAINS
Caradhras Pass
Paul Lasaine
This was one of a number of colour guides that Paul produced for Peter which captured how a scene should look so well that it became the template for the shot in the film (see below).

▲ **THE MISTY MOUNTAINS**
Caradhras Pass
Yanick Dusseault
This digital painting was used as a set extension to show the storm moving towards the Fellowship.

THE MISTY MOUNTAINS ▶
Caradhras Pass
Gus Hunter
This digital composite illustrates the point where the Fellowship, after leaving Rivendell, are beset by a furious storm summoned by Saruman, forcing them to enter Moria. Gus combined miniatures and painted elements — the model work is in the foreground, whilst the moutains in the distance are matte paintings.

MORIA

MORIA
The West-gate
Paul Lasaine
This colour scheme shows how the entrance to Moria would look when lit by the all-important moonlight. The tiny figures of the Fellowship can be seen to give an idea of scale.

MORIA
Exterior pencil sketches
Alan Lee
"The picture below was used to create the miniature for the outside of Moria. There's a shot almost identical to this sketch in the final movie. It is always satisfying to know you got something pretty much right the first time."

MORIA
The Lake
Paul Lasaine
By taking two frames from a panning shot of the lake and its environs, Paul has created all the backgrounds for this set-up, including the mountains, the cliffs etc. Then, to bring it all together, he has colour-graded the whole shot to make one smooth finished image.

MORIA
Mine-workings
Alan Lee
"One of my favourite drawings of the interior of Moria. This was created as a miniature and used in the shots of the Fellowship approaching the cemetery stairs."

MORIA
On the way to Balin's Tomb
Alan Lee
"These are sketches of various parts of the Mines of Moria. The one above is a chamber the Fellowship go through on their way towards Balin's Tomb, shortly after they actually enter the mine workings. The picture below takes place shortly afterwards, and shows the three forks that Gandalf faces before taking them into the tomb."

MORIA
Dwarrowdelf
Alan Lee
"The top picture is the Dwarrowdelf chamber, which is a
mainly computer-generated environment. The lowest
sections of the pillars were built for use in close-up action
with the Fellowship as the Orcs pursue them. The other
drawing is a design for the entrance chamber to Moria,
which the Fellowship discover to be full of corpses."

MORIA
Dwarrowdelf
Jeremy Bennett
These three pencil illustrations were done by Jeremy to show Peter Jackson how the sequences already filmed with the actors could be integrated with the as-yet undesigned Dwarrowdelf entrance and exit. Jeremy based the overall design on the work Alan Lee had already done with the pillars, as well as the floors and door bases that had been used on location.

MORIA
Dwarrowdelf
Jeremy Bennett
Because the Dwarrowdelf interior was almost entirely computer generated, Jeremy created these eight illustrations that form a storyboard to the sequence, to show how the lighting would work as the Fellowship flees from Balin's Tomb and out of Dwarrowdelf itself.

MORIA
Dwarrowdelf
Jeremy Bennett
A fully developed extrapolation of the smaller images on the
preceding page, this large painting shows the Fellowship
fleeing through Dwarrowdelf, illuminated not just by
Gandalf's staff but by the flame-red glow of the pursuing
Balrog.

MORIA
Khazad-dûm
Alan Lee

"These two drawings are of the part of Moria which lies between the Dwarrowdelf chamber and the bridge where Gandalf meets the Balrog. In the book you get the impression that they descend through tunnels, but there was an opportunity here for something quite spectacular which would allow us to see more of the ruined Dwarven city and the plunging depths below it. It was built as a miniature and Grant designed the set elements that were used in conjunction with it.

"This was an instance where Peter liked the first image so much (the one on the left) that all the subsequent drawings were just more detailed refinements for the model-makers."

MORIA
Khazad-dûm
Paul Lasaine and Gus Hunter

Taking a frame of the miniature bridge, Paul then worked
in the surrounding matte painting of the chasm to show what
might be developed in the background. These two versions
demonstrate potential alternate lighting effects.

   "For the shot at the bottom, Gus again took a frame of
the miniature, and this time used it to demonstrate to Peter
Jackson the lighting from the cavern area itself, based on
Paul's painting above.

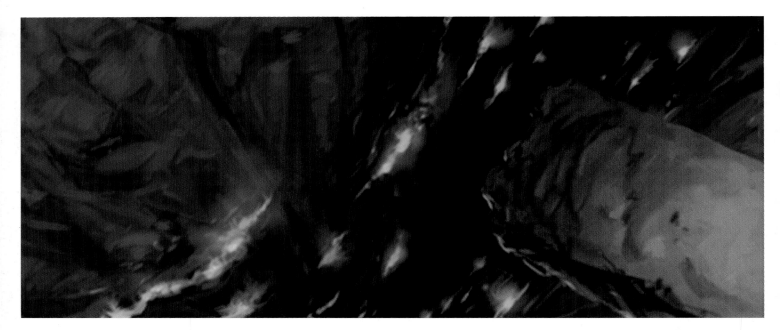

▲ **MORIA**
Khazad-dûm
Gus Hunter
Gus created two digital paintings to demonstrate what would be seen below during the fight between Gandalf and the Balrog, and where they were going as they fell. The top picture illustrates the cracks of lava and flame on the sides of the chasm, whilst the lower image shows the full fire pit.

► **MORIA**
Khazad-dûm
Gus Hunter
Taking Alan Lee's conceptual drawings as a starting point, Gus created these matte paintings using the miniature of the steps that had been created in the Weta workshops. The top composite was done to show how much flame and lava is visible in the cavern, and to give a feeling of depth, although it was important to hint at the bottomlessness of the cavern. The columns of the stairway actually go down further than the original frame of the miniature, and the base doesn't show lava so much as flame, rocks and smoke to imply that it's there, somewhere, far beneath the bridge. The lower shot offers an alternative to the first, but with richer flame effects to enhance the atmosphere.

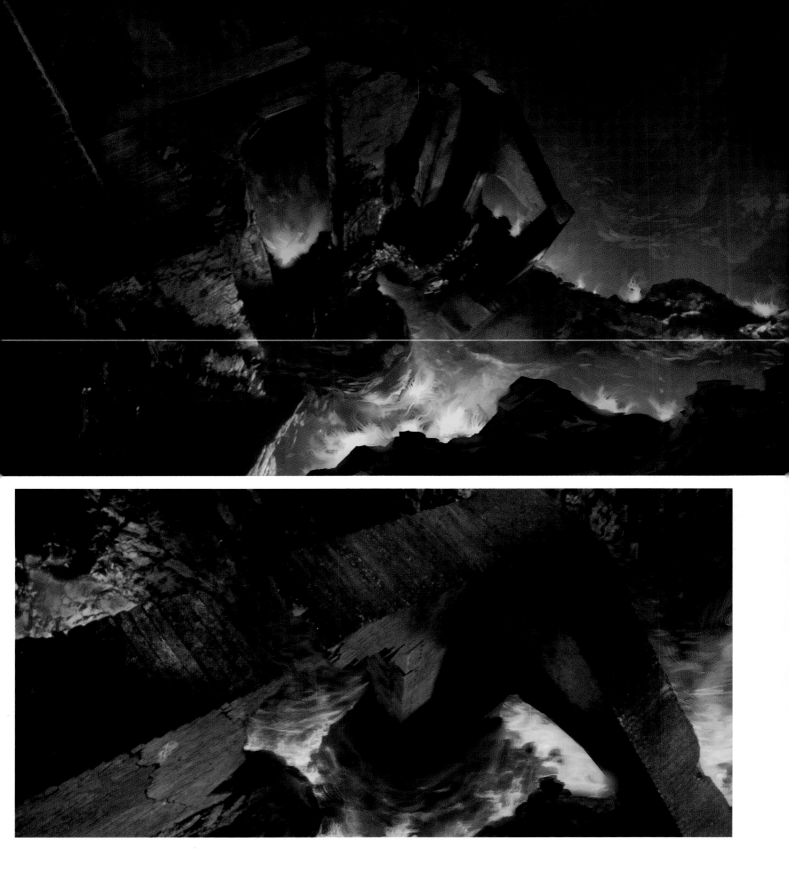

▲ **LOTHLÓRIEN**
The Valley
Roger Kupelian
Having just escaped some Orcs, Aragorn looks out towards Lothlórien Valley. The top frame shows what was shot on location, the lower is a temporary composite in which Roger has brought all the final elements together.

► **LOTHLÓRIEN**
Caras Galadhon
Wayne Haag
A composite of various live action shots, miniatures and matte paintings, showing the Fellowship high in the treehouses of the Elves.

LOTHLÓRIEN
The Glade
Max Dennison

For a sequence ultimately excised from the movie, this is the before and after digitally enhanced shots of the Fellowship going through the mallorn forest on their way to meet Galadriel for the first time. Note the spotlight which Max adapted as the beam of sunlight.

LOTHLÓRIEN
Tree concepts
Alan Lee

"These are some of many possibilities we offered up for the dwellings in Lothlórien. The model-makers, led by John Baster and Mary MacLachlan, would work directly from drawings like this, sometimes copying details as closely as possible and at others taking them just as a starting point, which they would expand on in a free-form way.

"Lothlórien, like most of the sixty-odd miniatures that were built at Weta for the movie trilogy, developed in quite an organic way, much as it would have done in reality. There are always design maquettes, and these are useful for Peter to work out the kind of shots he'd like to get, as well as sort out the scope and logistics of the miniatures. But the end result is down to the skill and artistry of those dedicated model-makers, and later to the craft of people like Alex Funke and the miniatures film unit."

LOTHLÓRIEN
Tree concepts
Alan Lee

"A lot of drawings are done in quite an exploratory way. I won't know exactly what I'm aiming for when I start. I'll begin at the bottom of the page and gradually work my way up, following the form of the tree and adding stairs, bridges and buildings as I go. It's really an elaborate doodle, but it's doodled in an Elven frame of mind.

"These drawings are shown to Peter, and his response may lead to further variations, or be a confirmation that we are on the right track. Peter liked the way the buildings had an almost flower-like look — as though they were delicately balanced on their branches."

LOTHLÓRIEN
Exterior view
Alan Lee

"These views of the Elven home were for the matte painters to establish the view from a distance. The one on the extreme left was done much earlier. I was just trying to work out how the trees might look from some distance. You didn't want to see the actual city inside too early." Yanick Dusseault's finished painting is far right. Ultimately, this scene was cut from the film.

▲ LOTHLÓRIEN
Galadriel and Celeborn's Chamber
Paul Lasaine

"This is a big painting of Lothlórien, the Elven city in the trees — possibly the first one I did as a detailed exploration of the colours we might use. It's primarily based on some of Alan Lee's drawings where he designed the architecture and even the trees themselves. From the very start Peter Jackson had this list of shots in his head that he was hoping would provide a good idea of what things would look like overall. This kind of thing was an inspiration to him and to everybody involved. Some of Lothlórien was so abstract, conceptually, as there wasn't going to be any set built, the actors would be working on blue screen all the time, so that's where a lot of these concept paintings were helpful to them. This was a full miniature with the characters digitally composited in, as the building was too big for many shots."

LOTHLÓRIEN
Exterior sketches
Alan Lee

"Ideas for other things would crop up while working on any particular subject, and on the drawing on the right are various designs for Nenya, Galadriel's ring. This was eventually designed and made by Jasmine Watson, the wardrobe department's jeweller."

LOTHLÓRIEN
Caras Galadhon
Paul Lasaine
"This look inside Celeborn's chamber shows the Fellowship arriving. It was developed from a sketch by Alan Lee. Alan's art was scanned and then painted over as a quick guide to colour and lighting for the miniature. So this mixes Alan's pencils, Photoshop and a live action inserted plate."

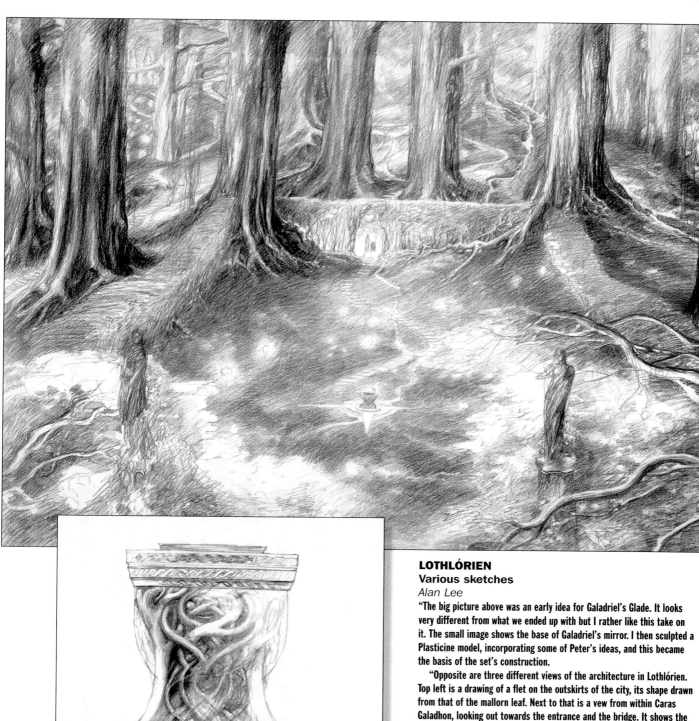

LOTHLÓRIEN
Various sketches
Alan Lee

"The big picture above was an early idea for Galadriel's Glade. It looks very different from what we ended up with but I rather like this take on it. The small image shows the base of Galadriel's mirror. I then sculpted a Plasticine model, incorporating some of Peter's ideas, and this became the basis of the set's construction.

"Opposite are three different views of the architecture in Lothlórien. Top left is a drawing of a flet on the outskirts of the city, its shape drawn from that of the mallorn leaf. Next to that is a vew from within Caras Galadhon, looking out towards the entrance and the bridge. It shows the route the Fellowship will take on their way up to the city. The largest picture is an idea for the gateway at the foot of the hill. We didn't use this in the end — sometimes we present ideas which, though everyone likes them, don't quite fit in with the way the scene has to work dramatically."

LOTHLÓRIEN
Galadriel's Glade
Paul Lasaine

"Above is a quick composite based upon footage that had been shot, to demonstrate colour and lighting, both of which are generic here. In the final shot, the background elements of the glade would be painted in.

"To the right is a colour key of the woods of Lothlórien, painted before filming began, which shows the level of light breaking through the trees."

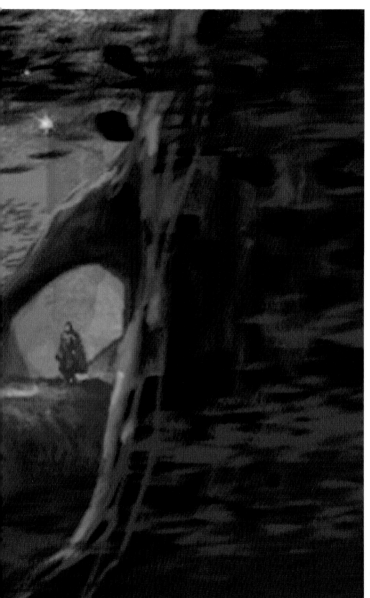

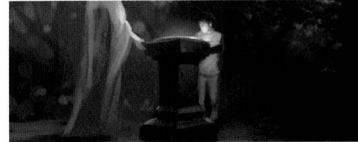

LOTHLÓRIEN
Galadriel's Glade
Paul Lasaine

Taking storyboards produced by Christian Rivers as a starting point, Paul created these conceptual studies to show both colour and the rippling effect of light shining up from the water in Galadriel's mirror.

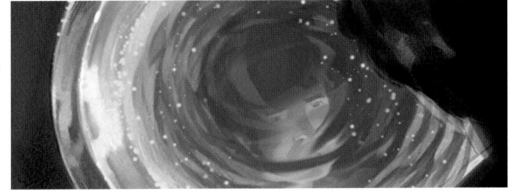

GALADRIEL'S GLADE

SCENE 150-12   BENNETT

GALADRIEL'S GLADE
Ruined Hobbiton
Jeremy Bennett
The top illustration is Jeremy's first pencil take on this sequence, the lower one a full colour version. It shows the mood and colour scheme intended for the scene as Frodo sees this possible future for his home. Jeremy cheated the landscape, compressing the buildings together to add to the desolation.

GALADRIEL'S GLADE
Ruined Hobbiton
John Howe
"Here is a vision of the Shire being destroyed. They built the miniature straight from this. And they built that crazy hill with all the pipes and that sort of mad, hellish mill. (Oh, and swimming across the bottom are little doodle eyes of Sauron. They ended up on the film crew's T-shirts.)"

▲ RIVER ANDUIN
Argonath Statues
Roger Kupelian
This temporary composite shot brings together all the elements of the scene — the matte backgrounds, the various rock faces, and the miniatures of the Pillars of the Kings themselves. Only the location footage of the North Island's Rangitikei River, doubling as the Anduin, is exactly as it was filmed on the day.

◄ RIVER ANDUIN
Argonath Statues
John Howe
"The Argonath. The finished ones in the movie were far more Roman-looking, but this early piece I did shows them looking more Northern European. Alan and I did sketches and they combined our two ideas but I have to say I wish they'd been closer to the sketches he did, rather than sort of between the two. I was very, very eager to have their feet in the water, to have the Argonath standing right over into the current so that the boats can go between their legs."

◄◄ RIVER ANDUIN
Argonath Statues
Paul Lasaine
On the previous page are three colour schemes produced by Paul, offering various colour palettes for consideration. This composition was also worked up into one of a number of possible poster ideas that he produced for Peter. It proved so popular that it was adapted into a finished piece of marketing artwork and used as a teaser poster.

RIVER ANDUIN
Nen Hithoel
Roger Kupelian
Another composite by Roger, this time combining the various elements with live footage of the Fellowship heading towards a fateful encounter at Amon Hen.

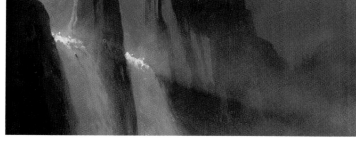

RIVER ANDUIN
Falls of Rauros
Paul Lasaine
"The paintings on the left are colour guides for Peter of the river itself, showing three different times of day. The two above are further down river, at the Falls of Rauros, and are views of Boromir's boat going over after he's been killed, with Aragorn and Gimli standing on the edge watching. It's a very heroic scene."

AMON HEN
The Seeing Seat
John Howe
Below is a detail from a concept painting of part of Amon Hen by John Howe, designed as a huge assemblage of Roman Temples. And left, a photo of the full-size Seeing Seat constructed for the location shooting.

AMON HEN
The Seeing Seat
Alan Lee
"A couple of roughs for the Seeing Seat. I had the idea of using these eagle motifs because of their excellent vision, symbolic of what Amon Hen's about."

AMON HEN
The Seeing Seat
Roger Kupelian
Below is a view of the Amon Hen ruins, but from a different angle. This is a composite painting only half-finished, showing a fraction of the entrance-way to the Seeing Seat.

AMON HEN
Frodo's visions
Paul Lasaine

"Peter requested these colour sketches early on, just to give him a few hints. They weren't done for colour specifically, but were to show the type of effects, one being the Eye of Sauron, the next one was Wraith World as Frodo first sees it, and then the Witch King's face. All of these went through quite an extensive development in terms of their look."

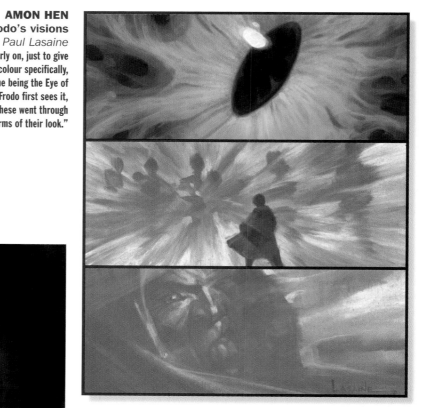

AMON HEN
Frodo's visions
Jeremy Bennett

Jeremy did this quick painting as an element for Gus Hunter to use for his sequence of visions (see above right). Once Gus had the image of Frodo in the Seeing Seat and had created the tunnel vision effect, he needed some images for Frodo to see. This was one of three paintings Jeremy did for that, this one showing a horde of battling Orcs swarming out of the Misty Mountains. The other two images Frodo sees are of the Cosair ships on the River Anduin and Mirkwood forest burning. These were ultimately cut from the movie.

AMON HEN
Frodo's visions
Gus Hunter

These are the first and last frames of the sequence in which Frodo sees into Wraith World after putting on the Ring. The point of these two designs was to illustrate how the tunnel vision effect would look on screen to display the sights that emerge. The effect uses tongues of flickering flame, acting like fingers, flowing outwards. The actual images from inside Wraith World are paintings by Jeremy Bennett — the first of the Dark Tower, the second of Sauron's Eye — that Gus composited in to the live action.

The image of the Eye of Sauron (far left) was based on Paul's colour sketch. Initially, animal eyes were used as a reference for the pupil but the pointed tips became more rounded as designs progressed, with the surrounding wreath adapted to appear as though in a heat haze. The first internet trailer showed the Eye with a double pupil, but Peter Jackson eventually settled on the image as it appears here.

RIVER ANDUIN ▶ ▶
Falls of Rauros
Jeremy Bennett

Jeremy's concept for the Falls of Rauros, which he knew would be made up of digital composites of waterfalls from a variety of locations in the finished movie.

▲ MORDOR
Emyn Muil
Paul Lasaine
The two pictures on this spread are amongst Paul's
favourites and were done deliberately to echo each
other, one from the start of the movie (the Shire)
and one from the ending (Mordor). The contrast is
not just between what the pictures show, but the
way the colours create mood and atmosphere.

► HOBBITON
The Shire
Paul Lasaine
"The main picture shows Frodo and Sam as they get their
first view of the mountains of Mordor. This is the point
where the good guys realize that all that was once familiar is
now behind them, and Mordor has begun creeping up like a
cancer to take over the world. The idea of doing contrasting
paintings was that they were going to be an exact
comparison, so you get this feeling of how far the Hobbits
have journeyed into the shadow during their travels."

▲ MORDOR
Gorgoroth Plains
Jeremy Bennett
In keeping with the colour scheme set up by Paul Lasaine, this is another interpretation of the vast battle sequence that takes place during the Second Age sequences. Jeremy had to turn this one around very quickly as it was required for a specially shot sequence to be put into the first trailer. It was used by the matte painters as a guide to the scale of the battle.

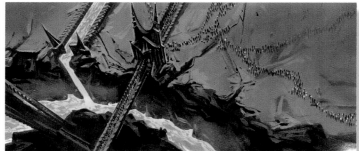

▼ MORDOR
Barad-dûr
Jeremy Bennett
Three separate frames from a long panning shot showing the
Orcs swarming towards the Barad-dûr bridge. The camera
pans past them and onto the Orcs who are rebuilding
Sauron's destroyed fortress. These were used as colour
guides and he added the Orcs to give the digital artists a
sense of scale and environment.

MORDOR ▶▶
Gorgoroth Plains
Paul Lasaine
"This conceptual image was produced as a first look at
the giant battle that happens in the flashback sequences
in the Second Age. Here we see Sauron casting an eye
over his troops — Peter Jackson wanted to get a feeling
of what it might look like when you have 600,000 troops
ready for war in Mordor. I used a different colour palette
for this one — avoiding the harsh browns and industrial
blacks of 'our' Mordor, this painting instead has cool
greys, magentas and a rather steely blue about it."

Costume

GANDALF
The Return to Bag End
John Howe
"This was a piece that was done when Peter had a presentation to make to sell the film in. He wanted something that showed off, again, the scale of Bag End and Gandalf and the hut and a bit of the Shire, you know ... Peter always wants to put thirty-five elements in each picture, which is a request I occasionally had some difficulty with! I was very happy with this cart, because it actually came out like that. It didn't come out blue in the film, but it came out very close to that. I'm not sure if the lamp survived the transition to film, but the cart certainly did."

FRODO
Costume design sketches
Ngila Dickson & Sylvana Sacco
"One thing that gave me nightmares was that, because you had a Hobbit of a normal height and of a film height — 4 foot 2 — you had to make sure that you could completely re-make the garment in scale. That meant you had to create, say, the different size buttons, and you had to redo every amount of stitching at its scale. You then had to have the fabric woven at both scales, so that the two would move the same on a small person as they do on a large one."

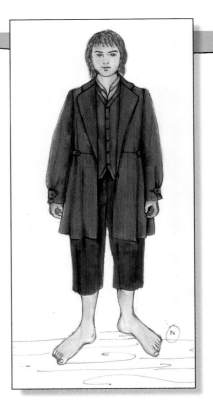

SAM
Costume design sketches
Ngila Dickson & Sylvana Sacco
"I think the Hobbits were the most straightforward characters to design. The first thing I did when I got the script was a little drawing of what I thought a Hobbit was, and in fact what the Hobbits finally ended up being wasn't that far from that."

MERRY & PIPPIN
Costume design sketches
Ngila Dickson & Sylvana Sacco
"First of all I went through the illustrations that Alan Lee had done. Then I looked at every picture anyone had ever done of Hobbits and came up with a set of descriptions for the Hobbits that stood me in good stead for the entire film. I wanted to create a sense that all of their clothes felt slightly off — like their trousers were too small, too short in the leg. And their sleeves were always too short. That just pulled everything back so that all the normal sort of stretching elements that you would have in clothing, we made them all slightly wrong."

BILBO BAGGINS
Costume design sketches
Ngila Dickson & Sylvana Sacco
"Bilbo, like the others, had to have this odd clothes sense. But I also wanted to set him apart a bit, express the notion he had travelled, met Elves, and was quite a wealthy hobbit. Consequently, his wardrobe has richer colours, and more lustrous fabrics. His red brocade waistcoat with its gold buttons is a direct nod to the text."

GANDALF

GANDALF THE GREY — AUGUST 99'

GANDALF THE GREY
Costume design sketches
Ngila Dickson & Sylvana Sacco
"Peter loved an image of Gandalf the Grey painted by John Howe. It was a beautiful image and a very powerful interpretation of Gandalf's character. It seemed like a real challenge to attempt to recreate it — so that's what we did. Of course, the hat was the real test..."

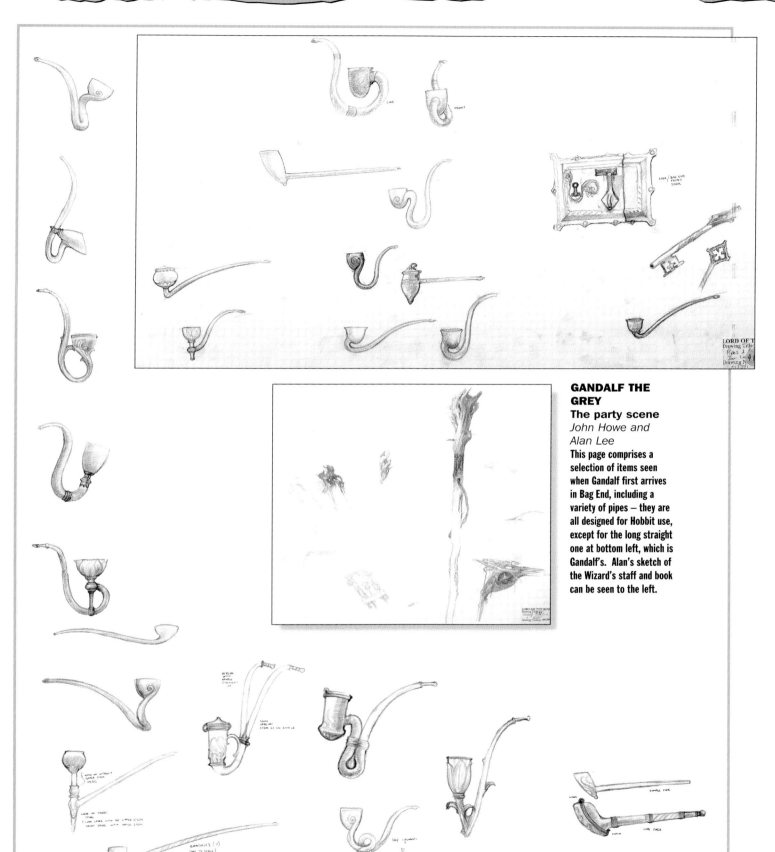

GANDALF THE GREY
The party scene
John Howe and Alan Lee

This page comprises a selection of items seen when Gandalf first arrives in Bag End, including a variety of pipes — they are all designed for Hobbit use, except for the long straight one at bottom left, which is Gandalf's. Alan's sketch of the Wizard's staff and book can be seen to the left.

ARAGORN

ARAGORN
Costume design sketches
Ngila Dickson & Sylvana Sacco

"We explored quite a few variations in the Aragorn costume. My original drawing was of a long forest-green leather coat. With that as a starting point, we tried different colours and lengths, different levels of decoration, added a vest... When we were happy with the final costume we realized we had travelled full circle and it was remarkably close to the original drawing!

Viggo joined the shoot very late and it was important that he was able to contribute to the costume. Luckily, it was one of those special wardrobe moments, when an actor puts on the costume and it's pretty well right. From that point on we worked closely with Viggo, adding the character's personal touches through stitching detail and breakdown elements. Viggo was very appreciative, which was fabulous."

Aragorn
Rivendell Council
Scene 92.5

BOROMIR
Costume design sketch
Ngila Dickson
"In the first design meeting about the Gondorians, they were described as the most ancient of civilizations, the Tolkien equivalent of Rome, Egypt or Byzantium. So the design motif reflects a little of these lost worlds, perhaps more towards Byzantium than the others."

Gimli son of Glóin

Falconer 98, Weta Workshop

"Gimli... wore openly a shirt of steel rings, for dwarves make light of such burdens..."

GIMLI
Costume design sketch
Daniel Falconer
Like a lot of the armour-clad characters, the earliest designs of Gimli were done by Weta's team rather than Ngila's. Here, Daniel Falconer has devised an idea for the son of Glóin but some time before the subsequent Dwarven design features had been established.

*A*RWEN

ARWEN
Costume design sketches
Ngila Dickson & Sylvana Sacco

"There are two types of Elves, the Lothlórien Elves, and the Rivendell Elves, which is what Arwen is. The basic view of the Rivendell Elves was that they were dark-haired, and the Lothlórien Elves were light. So we did tend to give the Rivendell Elves a richer, darker look. With Arwen it was important to go one step further, to show her empathy with the world of Men, and Aragorn in particular. So when you first meet Arwen she's in an Elven version of a riding outfit, practical and magical at the same time. The coat is a fine dove-grey leather, with a huge ornate silver buckle and Elven embroidery on the sleeve head. The underskirts are very light grey silk. Then, as the gravity of the future begins to weigh upon her, she retreats into the more traditional Elven clothing. We kept jewellery to a minimum, after she gives Aragorn the Evenstar; it was quite beautiful to have her unadorned."

The picture above right includes a detail for Arwen's quiver, designed by Daniel Falconer, which never made it into the film.

LEGOLAS

LEGOLAS
Costume design sketches
Ngila Dickson & Sylvana Sacco
"Legolas' costume was probably the most difficult to resolve. We had worked through many interpretations of this character, none of which were truly satisfying to Peter. Legolas has this extraordinary aloof beauty, and is the most athletic of the characters. We had to combine these. And, as always, when you return to a simpler design ethic often everything falls into place. We probably produced hundreds of variations on all the Elven characters, every time thinking we had found the perfect formula and then starting all over again. And we were doing all this against incredibly difficult deadlines. We were very determined to solve this."

ELROND

ELROND
Costume design sketches
Ngila Dickson & Sylvana Sacco
"The Elves were the most complex to design. There was little reference visually in Tolkien's text. But once we had found a motif based on leaf shapes and the fabrics (silks and fine wools all woven with metal thread) the costumes began to form in many variations."

GALADRIEL

Galadriel Lothlorien Design Concept · March 2000

GALADRIEL
Costume design sketches
Ngila Dickson

"Cate's casting as the character Galadriel allowed us to coalesce all the different ideas about the Elves into one, quite pure form. This creature had to be the ultimate Elf, the font of all wisdom. She needed to epitomize the grandeur, simplicity and elegance of these people. We kept the colours very pale, with silk velvets and very ornate and fine beading work. The jewellery was very specific. Her crown is the only one that incorporates gold with the silver. And the ring of Galadriel, desgined by our jeweller Jasmine Watson, is an extraordinary piece."

CELEBORN

CELEBORN
Costume design sketches
Ngila Dickson & Sylvana Sacco

"Because wardrobe had very little pre-production, initial complete drawings were confined to the Fellowship. Later, because of time pressures, drawings were often only a rough indicator — a construction brief for the Wardrobe Supervisor — allowing me to move the costume forward more quickly to the toile stage.

"By the time shooting started, we were on such a tight schedule, the drawing stage dropped out completely once we had a 'blueprint' for a civilization. We just started going straight into costume, making sometimes three options for each character because it was important Peter had a choice. Nothing was ever wasted in this process, the costumes not used by lead characters went straight into the extras wardrobe. It was very effective, really."

SARUMAN
Costume design sketch

Ngila Dickson & Sylvana Sacco

"The two wizards are the extremes of the Istari. Saruman so grand and fine and aloof, Gandalf the benevolent tramp roaming the countryside and in touch with its people. Saruman's costume draws reference from the Elves, in its fabric and style. It had to have an immense power to it, and I really wanted to accentuate Christopher Lee's height, a towering character, like Orthanc. In contrast, Gandalf's costume is very earthy and rumpled, the depth of his power hidden behind this genial outward appearance. The wizards have a deep connection to the Elves. There's a sense that the people who move in and around powerful magic understand the similar power of the Elves."

SARUMAN — OCTOBER 99

Armoury

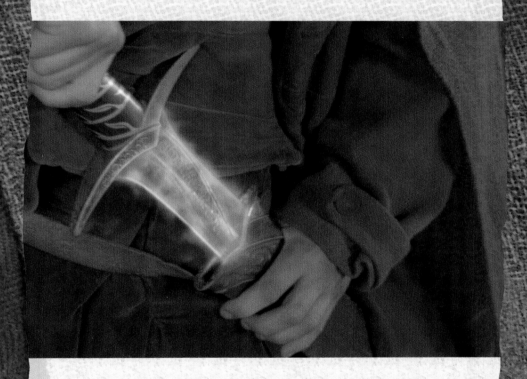

"This is an example of an idea to show Sting glowing. I took
the plate of the actor holding the sword (with blade whited
out in preparation for the addition of special effects) and
played with illuminating the lettering along the blade digitally.
The final version in the movie is slightly dimmer as Peter
Jackson wanted a little less intensity."
Paul Lasaine

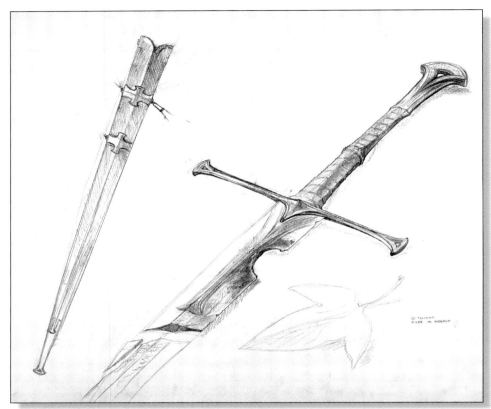

NARSIL
Pencil sketches
John Howe
A selection of ideas for Narsil, all of which feature the indentation made when Sauron's ringfinger is lopped off during the Second Age. John's final concept (inset left) was chosen and passed on to the Weta Workshop metal-workers to craft into the final prop.

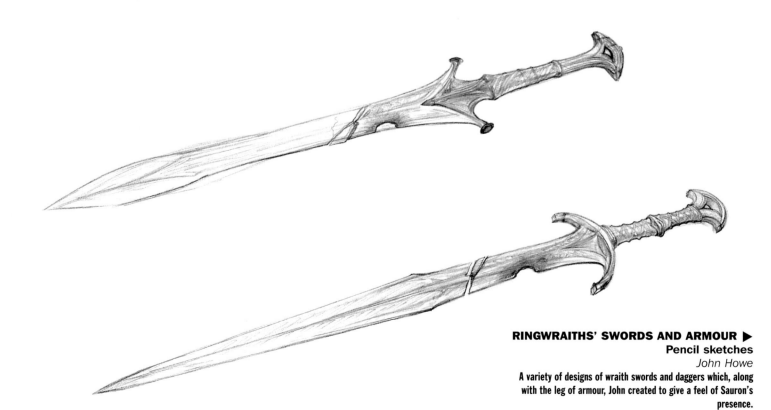

RINGWRAITHS' SWORDS AND ARMOUR ▶
Pencil sketches
John Howe
A variety of designs of wraith swords and daggers which, along with the leg of armour, John created to give a feel of Sauron's presence.

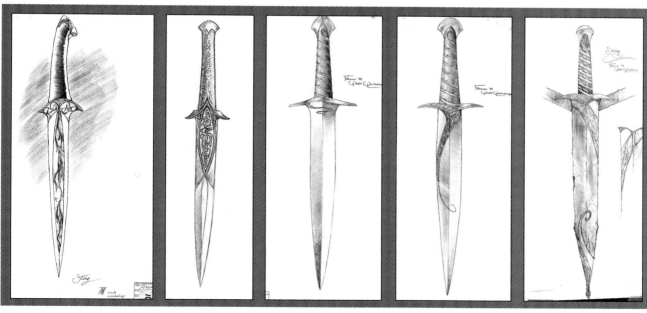

STING
Pencil sketches
Daniel Falconer

The left-hand Sting is an early design by Warren Mahy which Daniel adapted into his own. The third from the left established the shape of the blade whilst the next one worked in the Elven script that would run along the blade. The right-hand sketch shows almost the final design and utilised the scabbard.

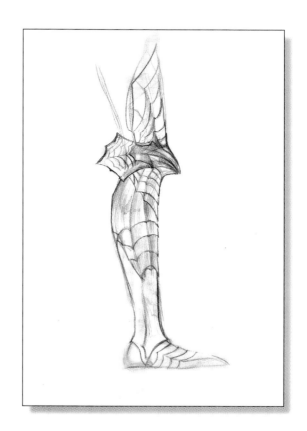

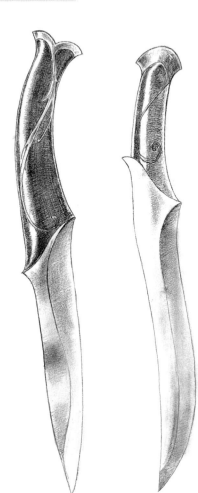

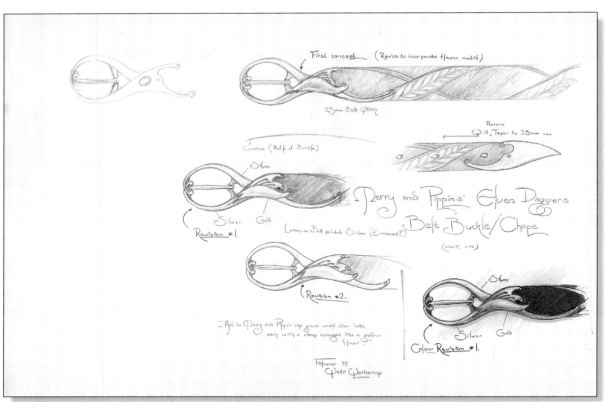

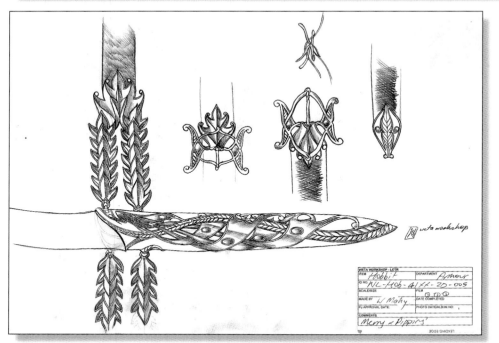

ELVEN DAGGERS
Pencil sketches

Daniel Falconer and Warren Mahy

When leaving Lothlórien, Merry and Pippin were given finely crafted Elven daggers by the Lady of the Wood, Galadriel. In designing the blades and their associated belts, chapes, buckles and scabbards, Daniel and Warren drew heavily from plant forms, a pervading theme in the Elven design style. The design as it appeared in the final film was a combination of both artists' work, featuring the buckle and belt designed by Daniel (top) and the scabbard designed by Warren (bottom).

ELENDIL
Early conceptual sketches
Ben Wootten

Ben adapted Daniel Falconer's original idea (see bottom sketch) which made use of the feathered motif in the cloak to mirror the designs on the helmet. Taking this through another couple of stages, Ben ended up with what was, bar one or two minor costume adjustments, the final Second Age image of Elendil (largest figure). Daniel Falconer designed buckle and chape variations to enable Elendil to carry Narsil on his belt, although these were not used in the final film.

Elendil's Belt Buckle/ Chapes for Narsil

Seven Holey Stars

Elendil (Alternative)

Falconer '99.
Weta Workshop

MITHRIL SHIRT

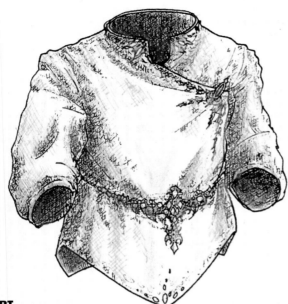

"...He unwound several folds of cloth, and held up a small shirt of mail. It was close woven and supple almost as linen, of many rings, cold as ice, and harder than steel. It shone like moonlit silver, and was studded with white gems. With it was a belt of pearl and crystal..."

The Fellowship of the Ring.

MITHRIL SHIRT
Early pencil sketches
Daniel Falconer
This important part of Frodo's costume went through a number of revisions, of which these are amongst the earliest.

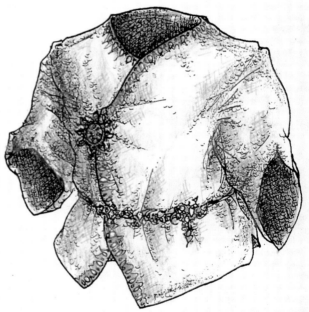

D. Falconer 98.
Weta Workshop

WETA WORKSHOP - LOTR		
ITEM *Hobbit.*		DEPARTMENT *Armour.*
ID NO. *MX-Hob-4/xx-2D-010.*		
SCALE/SIZE	FILM ① ② ③	
MADE BY *D Falconer*	DATE COMPLETED	
PJ APPROVAL DATE:	PHOTO DATE/ALBUM NO:	
COMMENTS		

GIL-GALAD
Early conceptual designs
Various artists

Daniel Falconer developed concepts for Gil-galad's crown (top left) and his battle armour (main image). Gil-galad's final crown as it is briefly glimpsed in the film was designed and built by Jasmine Watson. The colour scheme was drawn from the heraldry and colours of the generic High-Elven armour but was intensified to enable the character to stand out in the battle scenes. The two bottom Gil-galad figures by Ben Wootten (left) and Daniel (right) were variations on the same theme. Daniel's was the final approved design as it appeared in the film. Warren Mahy created the Second Age weaponry for Gil-galad's troops as well as the encasing armour worn by the army in battle (top right).

Elrond, (armour design concept)
Herald to King Gil-galad, Last
King of the
Elves in Middle-
Earth

ELROND
Armour design
Daniel Falconer
In this early concept for Elrond's Second Age armour
(seen in the Prologue sequence), Daniel's colour scheme
was drawn from Tolkien's own heraldry designs for the
Elves. In this drawing, Elrond wears the blue and gold of
his Lord, Gil-galad, befitting his role as Herald to the
King.

D.Falconer 99.
Weta Workshop

ELVEN INSIGNIA
Colour designs
Daniel Falconer
These badges were used to represent the various Elven armies that might appear in the Second Age sequences. Gil-galad's was a slight reworking of the one Tolkien himself created and similarly both the Houses of Elrond and Galadriel borrowed elements from his concepts for their respective fathers, Eärendil and Finarfin. The other designs were entirely Dan's inventions although clearly in keeping with the others. The designs were intended to appear on the breasts of the Elves' armour and were also incorporated by the Art Department for use in their Elven banners.

Houses of :

Gilgalad

Elrond
(from Earendil)

Galadriel
(from Finarfin)

Cirdan

Glorfindel

Falconer 98
Weta Workshop

ELVEN INSIGNIA

LEGOLAS' QUIVER

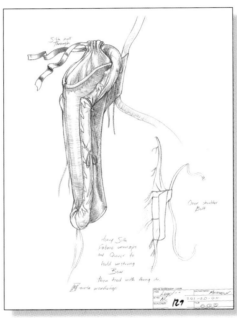

LEGOLAS' QUIVER
Colour and pencil sketches
Warren Mahy

"These are various sketches by myself and Dan Falconer. In the film, Legolas has two different quivers. The first, based on my drawing (far left, top), we called his Mirkwood quiver. The second is given to him by the Elves of Lothlórien. Dan's peacock-motif design was chosen for that one. The final prop differed slightly from the approved drawing (far left, bottom), being darker and missing the internal arrow bag. The finished props were made by a bow and arrow maker in Wellington, and they are of a pretty sturdy wood although I'm not sure what the wood is. They used proper feathers from turkeys and pheasants for Legolas' arrows, but for the rest they used synthetic feathers. The arrows actually had a proper head on them. Nice and sleek and fast so if they hit something, or someone, they'd go straight in. Some arrowbolts were really heavy, and you can imagine them breaking bones on the way through rather than just bouncing off the costumes..."

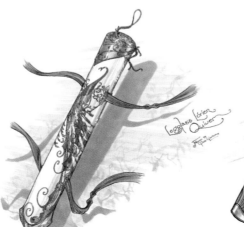

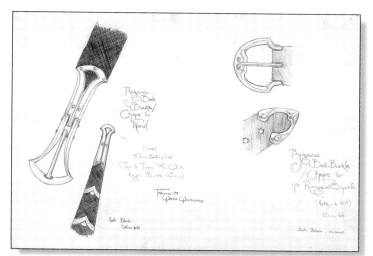

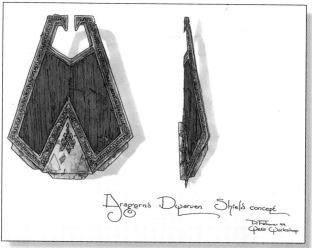

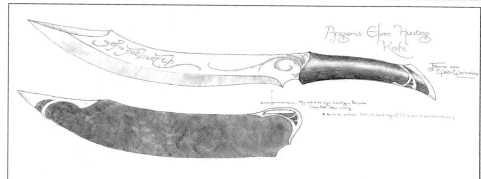

ARAGORN'S ACCESSORIES
Pencil sketches
Daniel Falconer

The chape and buckle (top left) are for Aragorn's belt and are used for attaching both Narsil and his Ranger's sword. The Dwarven shield (above) comes from a dropped scene, when Aragorn discovers it lying within the Mines of Moria. The long hunting knife (left) is a gift from the Elves and has a Sindarin inscription, to imply its great age and importance. It reads "foe of Morgoth's realm".

BOROMIR'S SHIELD AND BELT
Pencil sketches
Daniel Falconer

Daniel's initial design for the shield underwent very few alterations, just the addition of a pair of wings and seven stars to the boss decoration. The belt designs were for Boromir's sword-strap and shield-strap.

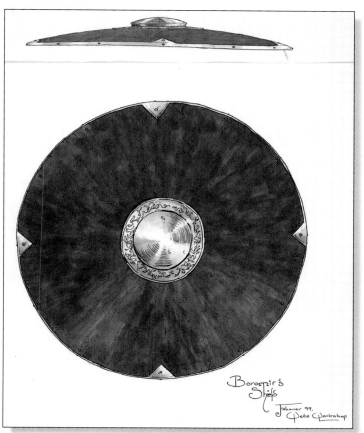

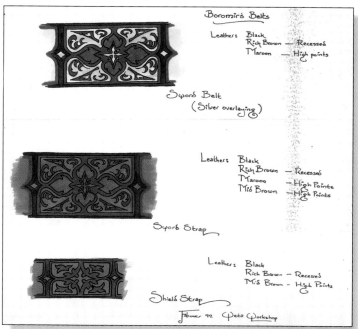

▲ **DWARVEN AXES**
Pencil sketches
Warren Mahy

"Because of the Dwarven architecture, a lot of the actual design elements were already done. We took shapes based on the architecture from Dwarrowdelf and Moria, and put it into the Dwarven weapons. A lot of the axes you see in Balin's tomb are all from that concept. It's the same for the helmets in the tomb, and Gimli's helmet: all the same sort of shape, all very square."

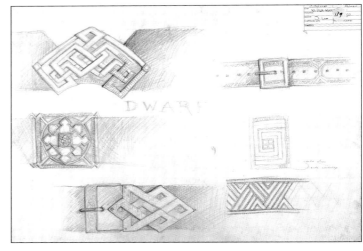

▶ **DWARVEN BELTS**
Pencil sketches
Sacha Lees

Various artists contributed to the design of the Dwarves. Sacha's belts and their buckles again derived from a lot of the already conceived architecture seen around Balin's tomb.

▶ **DWARF LORDS**
**Conceptual
sketches**
Daniel Falconer
To show some early ideas
for the prosthetics that
could be used on the actors
portraying the Seven Dwarf
Lords, Daniel Falconer drew
this collection of potential
Dwarven faces.

▼ **DWARVES**
Conceptual pencil sketches
Various
The two sketches of Dwarves at the bottom of the previous
page are by Warren Mahy, who used a series of geometric
shapes to suggest the precision and solidity of the Dwarven
armour. The drawings below by various artists all contain
elements that were incorporated into the final design aesthetic established for the Dwarves; from left: drawings by
Sourisak Chanpaseuth, Daniel Falconer and Warren Mahy.

SAURON

LORD OF THE
Drawing Title:
Sauron
Drav 424 nber:

SAURON
Original sketches
John Howe (insets by Warren Mahy)
"This was done a long time before we started filming. It's one of my earliest ideas for Sauron and his armour — I wanted to devise an armour that would work, that the Dark Lord could actually wear and have battles in but still be very spiky, extravagant and gothic."

SAURON
Pencil sketches
Warren Mahy

"For all the Mordor stuff, we went with dark iron. It was all very intricate without it looking like it was robotic. The same with Sauron's armour: it's quite tight, quite form-fitting, to try and convey the idea that Sauron and the wraiths are really skeletal. Sauron's armour was pushed and pulled over time as we could never quite work out what worked for the Second Age sequences and what would work best for any Third Age appearances: it was a really fluid process, but very constructive. One great thing about Weta Workshop was that we had a leather room — where they made the leather costumes — and similarly an armoury, where they made everything in metal. It all felt as well as looked real, which is what Richard Taylor wanted, because it gave the actors a real feel for who they were playing. Sauron's helmet went through a variety of designs, as seen in these sketches by Warren Mahy. The final version seen in the film was designed by Alan Lee. The mace at the top is the final version — we had lots of different ideas for that, and people were wondering whether that and the armour were supposed to be as old as Sauron, or whether he had had his armourers make new weapons. I think in the end we decided that it was more likely that it's very old, but he's probably taken as much care of it all as he can."

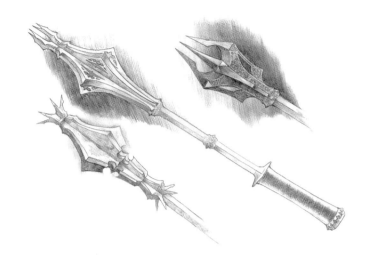

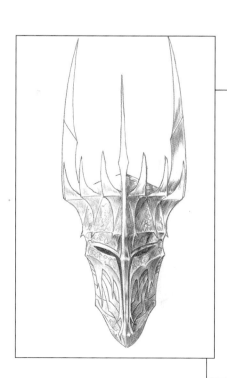

SAURON
Detail for armour
Christian Rivers

Whilst these pencil sketches for the armour and helmets were by Warren Mahy, who was charged with designing the overall Sauron concepts, Christian Rivers submitted a colour detail for the Sauron cape on the left. Although such a sequence isn't in the story itself, the two conceptual illustrations by Warren showing Sauron throttling an Orc minion and burning an enemy (above right and opposite) were done to give not only an idea of the height of Sauron in his armour, but also to contrast the cruel majesty of the character.

Creatures

"The hardest work by far was simply to come to that point where you can say, 'The design is finished', because you never quite want to let something go, because even though it looks good, you might say 'One more day's work', and the next day you get something better. So there always has to be that point where you say, 'Okay, this is what the Balrog is going to look like, it's finished'. A lot of my energy and time was spent handling that process and making sure that I was happy with what we finally decided to sign off on."

Peter Jackson

ORCS

ORCS
Early pencil sketches
Alan Lee

"Peter and Richard were keen on creating distinctly different breeds of Orcs, so that we wouldn't just have the same nasty little guys turning up in all three movies. So we have Mordor Orcs from the prologue, Moria Orcs and so on.

The final look of the Orcs had more to do with the armour and weapons the Weta team designed, and with the skilful use of digital eye-replacement."

▶ **MORIA ORCS**
Maquette
Ben Wootten
This maquette was designed when the intention was to create the Orcs digitally and thus didn't need to conform to human proportions, which would have given them a far more animalistic look which Peter Jackson liked.

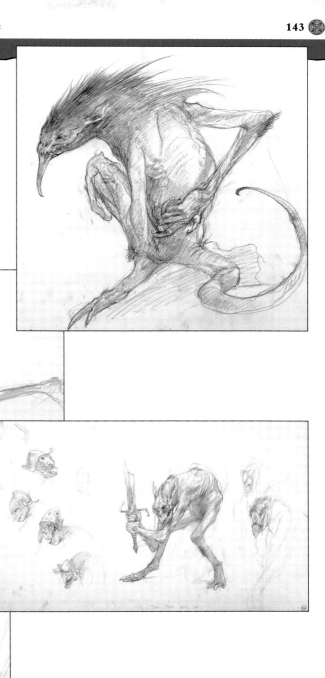

ORCS
Pencil sketches
John Howe

"The Orcs were a curious brief because it went round and round in the workshop. There wasn't too much discussion on the other Orcs, because they were sort of a junkyard Samurai kind-of Orc — everything goes armour-wise — but Peter wanted something special for the Orcs of Moria. And as time passed, the designs went off on these incredible tangents, away from humanoid towards goodness knows what."

 **MORIA ORC**
Maquette
Jamie Beswarick
Another early concept for the Orcs, again intended for digital rendering rather than being played by an actor.

▶ ORCS
Concept sketches
Various

(Clockwise from right) Johnny Brough's early concepts for the Orcs of Moria. The bottom left facial design in the inset closely resembled the final version which featured digital enlargement of the actors' eyes. Daniel Falconer's loping figure, carrying the crude staff, was again an early idea, to be realized via CGI. Both Christian Rivers' and Warren Mahy's sketches were similarly intended for digital rendering, particularly in light of Warren's insectoid body stance.

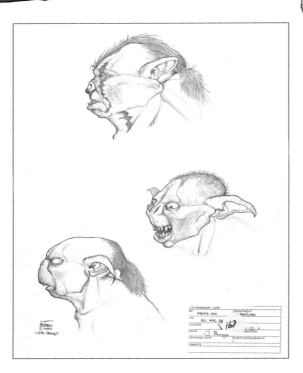

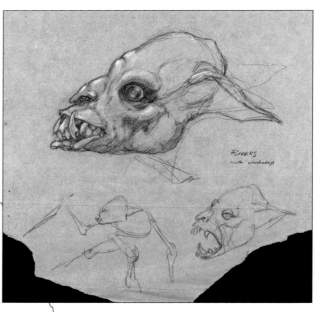

▶ ORCS
Maquette
Another early creation from Weta Workshop that focused in on the idea that they would have highly developed sensory perception, but it was abandoned quite early on.

▼ ORCS
Concept sketches
Various
Two alternative ideas for Moria Orcs. The one on the left by Ben Wootten is entirely animalistic, intended for digital creation, whilst Daniel Falconer's on the right is closer to that which was used in the film, as a face mask for an actor with digital eye enlargement. This drawing offered an alternative eye colour to that which was used.

ORCS
Armour design
Daniel Falconer

For this Moria Orc, Daniel designed armour to be constructed from wood, polished and laid over light steel frames. This meant that, with lightweight armour, along with unencumbered toes, the climbing of trees and pillars could be easily achieved. Another early Moria Orc concept (opposite), this idea didn't make it to the film. Again, he was designed to be realized via CGI. He carries a shield covered with straw dipped in oil and set alight. This would serve as both a lantern and also a weapon during battle.

▶ ORCS
Concept sketch
Warren Mahy

Another variant on the non-human Moria Orc design, wearing clothing that suggests they are more comfortable in the darkened halls of Dwarrowdelf than the brightness of the outside areas.

ORCS
Concept sketch
Warren Mahy
A version of the Moria Orc with armour and weapon. This still had some way to go before becoming the final Moria creature.

ORCS
Concept sketches
Various
The Orc at the top right, by Christian Rivers, was originally designed as a Moria Orc but was reused as a Mordor Orc. The same is true of Warren Mahy's Orc bottom left. The main image was created by Daniel Falconer specifically as a battle Orc, but again at a stage when the Orcs were to be realized digitally.

ORCS
Concept sketches
Various

Daniel Falconer designed several Moria Orc concepts with a range of varying armour styles (top right and bottom left). The bottom left Orc carries a weapon designed to snare and tangle foes. The central Orc, by Warren Mahy, is a very early Moria design when they were still being referred to in the script as Goblins. The maquette at bottom right was briefly approved as the look for the Orcs of Moria when it was intended that these would be realized entirely through CGI.

▲ **ORCS**
Digital composite
Mel James
Mel has created this image of a well-populated battlefield for Peter Jackson to examine, as an example of how such a sequence could look. Created using Photoshop, the image was a mixture of photographed Weta Workshop maquettes and a scanned New Zealand background landscape.

ORCS
Maquettes
Various
Moving away from his pencils and paints, John Howe crafted the Moria Orc below left and this design was used in the finished film. Below is Daniel Falconer's maquette of a much earlier Orc design, featuring armour made from scavenged materials. The hook on its back was designed to carry a lantern. The Orc on the next page, sculpted by Johnny Brough, is much closer to the final design of the Moria Orc heads.

D. Falconer 98.
Weta Workshop

◀ **ORCS**
Concept sketch
Daniel Falconer
Aspects of this armour design were used in Orc armour
but in fact this picture began life as an early idea of some
Uruk-hai armour, when the concept of the Uruk-hai's
distinctive look had yet to be determined.

▶ **ORCS**
Concept sketch
Daniel Falconer
A much later design, this Mordor Orc
features many components that would find
their way into various Orc costumes.

URUK-HAI

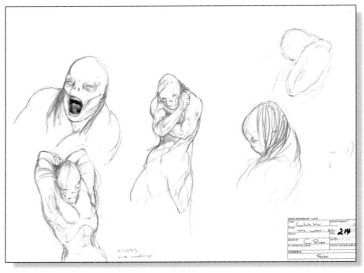

URUK-HAI BIRTHING
Concept sketches
Various

These images are by a variety of Weta's conceptual artists, showing how this scene might look. Warren Mahy's (left, top and bottom) show an Uruk-hai emerging from its sac, whilst between them is Daniel Falconer's idea for the sac as it opens. To the right, at the top of the page, are some ideas by Christian Rivers showing the newly hatched Uruk-hai acclimatising, whilst at the bottom is Ben Wootten's version of the sac itself. Opposite is a maquette of a new-born Uruk-hai getting to its feet, sculpted by Jamie Beswarick.

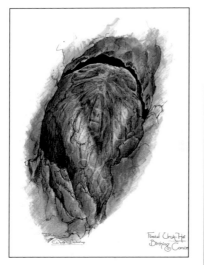

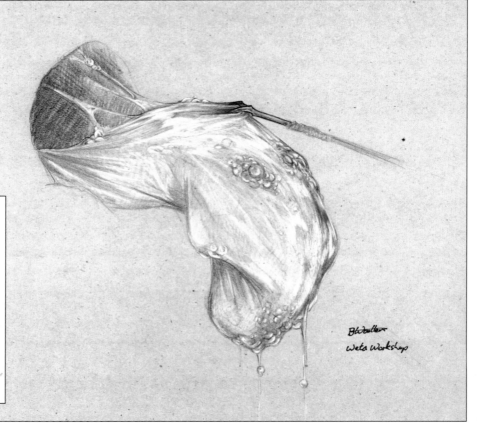

URUK-HAI WOODSMEN
Concept sketches
Warren Mahy

Both of these illustrations were used to demonstrate the tools and clothing worn by the Uruk-hai that chopped down the trees surrounding Orthanc. In the end, these designs weren't used as the job fell to Orcs, leaving the Uruk-hai purely as warriors.

URUK-HAI
Armour sketches
Christian Rivers and Warren Mahy
The collections to the left (at the top is Christian's, the lower one is Warren's) are early ideas for Uruk-hai armour, focusing on the covering of their faces. The larger illustration by Christian is a very early idea, looking quite sophisticated and featuring Saruman's white hand on the breastplate.

URUK-HAI
Head sculptures
*Ben Wootten and Jamie
Beswarick*
The top three maquettes (the bald one
at the top is Jamie's) are just some of
the many different ideas that were
proposed for the Uruk-hai faces. The
large picture bottom left, by Jamie
Beswarick, is actually the very first
piece of sculpture done for the trilogy of
movies. The irony being that the final
Uruk-hai design used in the movie went
very closely back to this one.

URUK-HAI
Concept sketches
*Daniel Falconer and
Christian Rivers*
Two very early sketches
to show the facial
characteristics of the
Uruk-hai, done before any
maquettes were created.
The top on is by Daniel, the
collection of four alternates
by Christian.

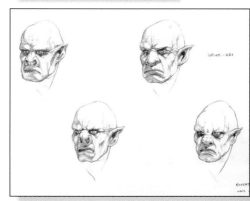

URUK-HAI
Armour concept
Christian Rivers

An early Uruk-hai design, seen here menacing a Hobbit, probably Merry or Pippin. The armour design was considered too refined looking and too evocative of a high-fantasy aesthetic. The design style established for all the races of Middle-earth came to reflect a greater emphasis on historical realism.

TROLLS

STONE-TROLL
Concept statue
Jamie Beswarick

As a nod to the continuity of the story from The Hobbit, the Hobbits and Strider come across the three trolls during their journey in The Fellowship of the Ring. Jamie worked with Plasticine in order to capture the correct texture of the troll, one of three tricked into turning to stone by Gandalf in Trollshaw Wood some years earlier while they argued over who was going to cook Bilbo and the Dwarves.

STONE-TROLL
Concept statue
Bill Hunt

As with the troll above, this is Bill's take on one of the trio. Head of Weta, Richard Taylor, considered the Stone-trolls to be one of the more delightful references to The Hobbit. Although never referred to in the film, fans will recognize the Trolls as those turned to stone in Bilbo's earlier adventure. The designs were loosely based on an Alan Lee painting from the illustrated edition of The Lord of the Rings.

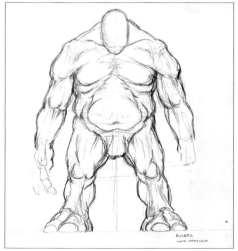

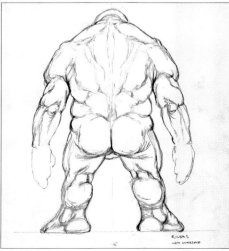

CAVE-TROLL
Early designs
Ben Wootten and Christian Rivers

Christian's pencil sketches and Ben's head sculpture were approved after a number of attempts, as the sequence featuring the creature is one of the most important in the movie. Peter described to the Weta team how he wanted the cave-troll to look. "Like an innocent child - only ten feet tall!", was his affectionate description. Richard Taylor felt that "at the end of the day, you'd probably get along quite well with the troll, the only trouble being when he gets pissed off he smashes the house up! You're drawn to feel empathy for him by the time he finally dies, because the righteous Fellowship have to deal extreme death, extreme punishment to save the quest. I like to think that you're drawn to be a little bit reflective about the fact that they have had to do that."

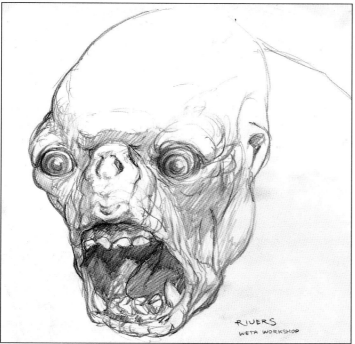

CAVE-TROLL
Conceptual designs
Christian Rivers and Ben Wootten
Working from the scanned digital model of the approved troll, Christian explored facial expressions, in this case a roar. Christian also drew the very first cave-troll concept back in 1997 (below right). Prior to the decision on the final facial design of the troll, Ben Wootten explored a variety of different face concepts (below left).

Jamie Beswarick's design maquette for the troll features overleaf, painted by Ben Wootten.

◀ **CAVE-TROLL**
Pencil sketch
John Howe
"A couple of cave-trolls! This was after the event, actually, because the cave-trolls had been designed by the time Alan and I arrived so all we saw were the finished full-sized maquettes. So this was just me playing around because, just for fun, I wanted to draw trolls!"

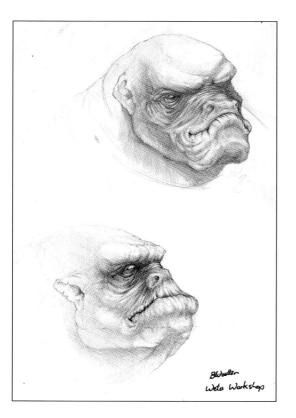

The WATCHER IN THE WATER

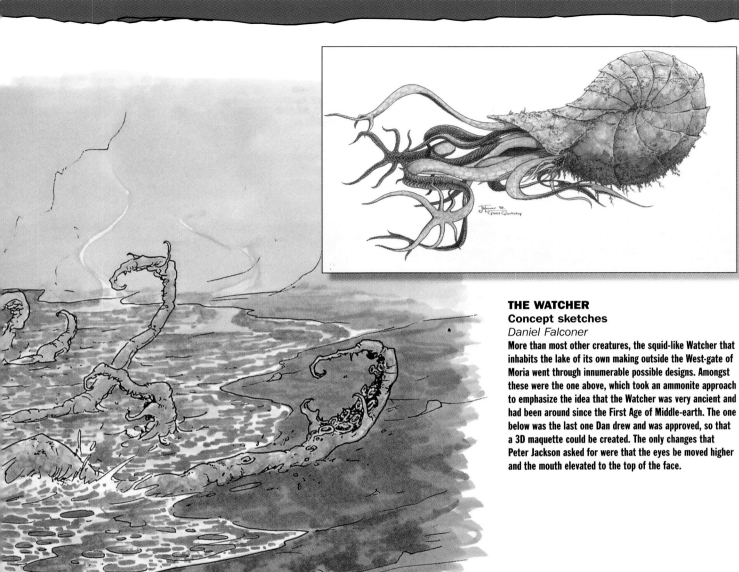

THE WATCHER
Concept sketches
Daniel Falconer

More than most other creatures, the squid-like Watcher that inhabits the lake of its own making outside the West-gate of Moria went through innumerable possible designs. Amongst these were the one above, which took an ammonite approach to emphasize the idea that the Watcher was very ancient and had been around since the First Age of Middle-earth. The one below was the last one Dan drew and was approved, so that a 3D maquette could be created. The only changes that Peter Jackson asked for were that the eyes be moved higher and the mouth elevated to the top of the face.

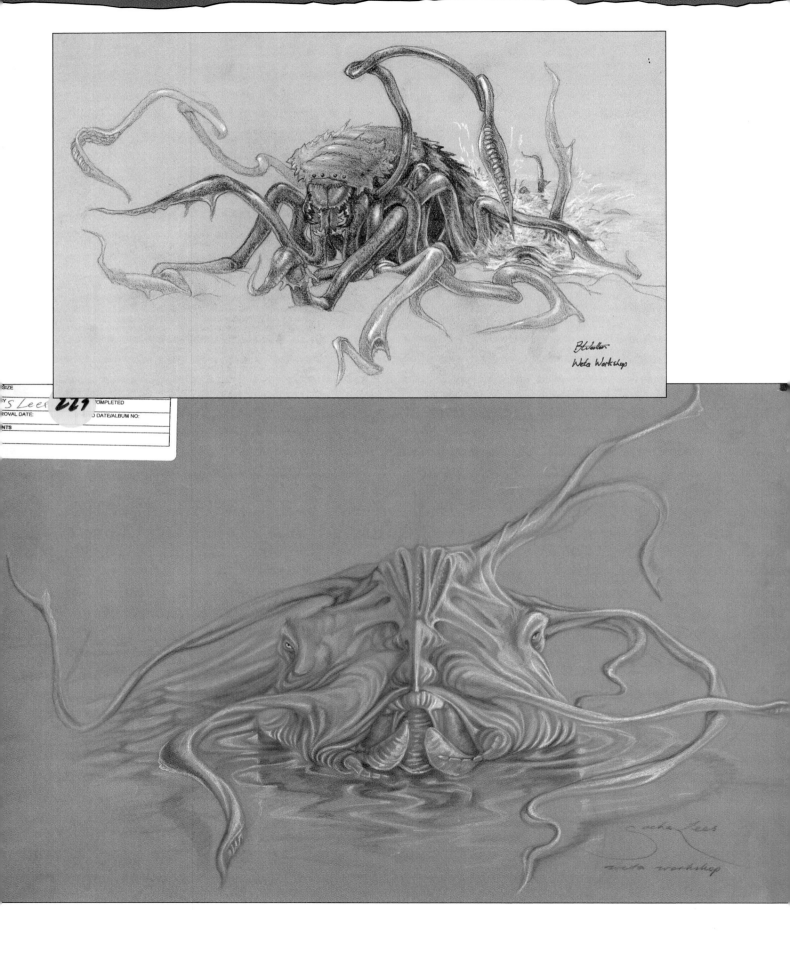

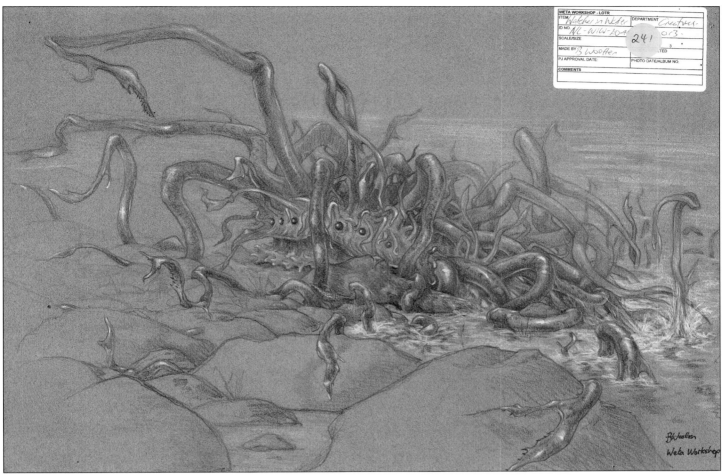

THE WATCHER
Concept sketches
Various

Beginning top left, Ben Wootten's early Watcher concept was very crustacean-based, while Sacha's drew upon a very deep-sea look for this concept of hers (below left). The image above by Ben Wootten drifted more to an anemone look, whilst the one below, by Warren, emphasizes the mouth and tentacles to create a nightmarish vision. Once the creature design was locked down, Christian Rivers produced the production illustration (overleaf) based on the Watcher design by Daniel Falconer.

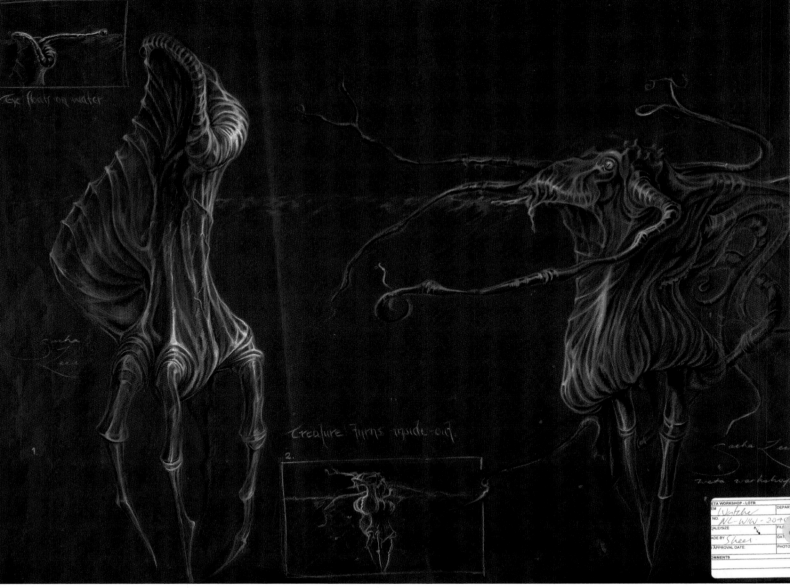

▲ **THE WATCHER**
Concept sketches
Sacha Lees
This possible idea of the Watcher demonstrates how, by manipulting its fluid-filled body, the creature is reversible.

THE WATCHER
Concept sketches
Daniel Falconer and Warren Mahy
Daniel's Watcher, above, was rejected as it appeared to be too deep-sea in origin rather than a creature that might live in a lake. Warren's, right, shows the possible scale of the Watcher against the Hobbits below.

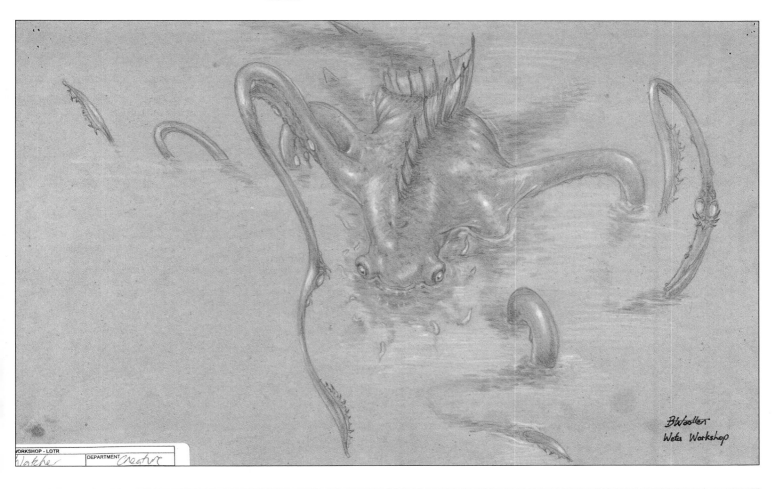

WORKSHOP - LOTR | DEPARTMENT Creature

THE WATCHER
Concept sketches
Ben Wootten
The two Watchers here represent ideas that were put forward which moved away from the squid concept and became, in the top, more unique to Middle-earth, while the lower one seems more akin to a cuttlefish.

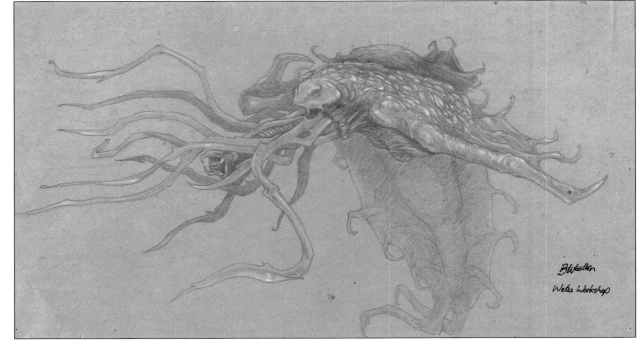

RINGWRAITHS

RINGWRAITHS
Wraith world concept
Paul Lasaine
According to Weta's Richard Taylor, the 'real' Kings (as opposed to their Black Rider forms) were "a very interesting design problem. How do you re-invent zombies? Well, they're not zombies, they're a spiritual emanation, but they are still a solid, prosthetic glue-on job on an actor's face that emulates decay, age and a sapping of spirit. We wanted to bring a new bent to the look of the spiritual world, so Peter Jackson suggested that we imagined they'd been sucking on lemons for a thousand years, and that's exactly what we went for."

RINGWRAITH AND HORSE
Pencil sketches
John Howe and Alan Lee

"These are a couple of pictures of the Witch-king and the wraith horses. The idea at one point was to have the horses created digitally, so there was the full excitement of designing something completely new. I was really happy with the sketch showing the entire creature, because it's a horse and it's not a horse — I wanted something very disturbing, so the underbelly is actually that of a bull. And the legs are very much more of, well, I was thinking along the lines of a large predatory cat. The head is a bit small. It was wonderful to design a new breed of horse — but in the end it turned out that to have a real horse was much more economical. That noseguard at the bottom right was an idea Alan came up with to add to the malevolent look."

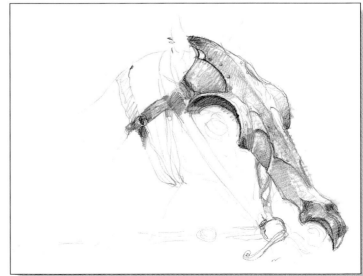

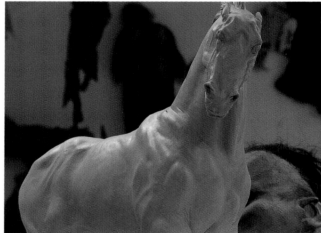

RINGWRAITHS
Wraith World Facial Concept and Horse Maquettes
Jamie Beswarick and Ben Wootten
Above, an early concept for the wraiths' faces as they appear to Frodo in the Weathertop sequence. Working from John Howe's sketch, Ben developed the wraiths' horses in 3D Plasticine maquettes below.

RINGWRAITHS
Concept sketches
Christian Rivers

A lot of discussion went into the wraith horses — should they be as evil as the Ringwraiths, or terrified and tortured, being driven against their will? Similarly, it was wondered if they ought to be a new breed of horse previously unseen. Pure black horses are quite rare and in a number of shots, the horses' traditional white ankles had to be digitally coloured to match the rest of their bodies.

RING WRAITHS

RIVERS
WETA WORKSHOP

THE WORKSHOP - LOTR
ITEM BALROG. DEPARTMENT Creature
ID NO. Mx-BAL-2005-2D-009.
SCALE/SIZE FILM ① 2 3
MADE BY C.Rivers DATE COMPLETED
PJ APPROVAL DATE PHOTO DATE/ALBUM NO
COMMENTS
278

RIVERS '97
WETA WORKSHOP
BALROG CONCEPT

THE BALROG
Concept sketch
Christian Rivers
One of the earliest ideas for the Balrog. Christian initially went down the route of a man-shaped creature with wings of flame.

▶ THE BALROG
Concept sketch
Ben Wootten
This idea saw a much more reptilian look coming to the fore, but with the mane of fire that would stay right through to the final creature. Ultimately, the Balrog was realized more through a series of maquettes than on paper, although John Howe's influence can be seen throughout the process.

THE BALROG ▶▶
Production illustration
Christian Rivers
Christian created this piece (overleaf) to show how the Balrog would be first seen in its entirety at the collapsing bridge of Khazad-dûm.

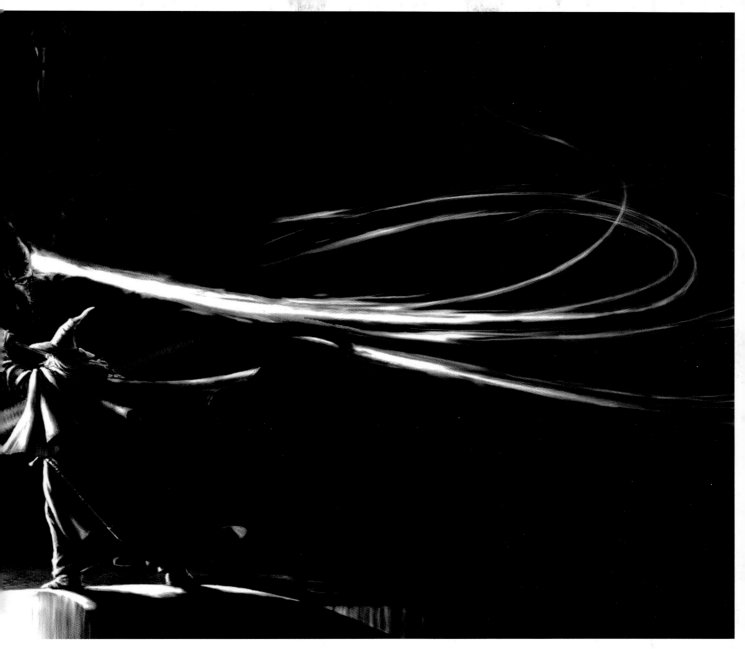

THE BALROG
Concept sketch
Shaun Bolton
Shaun depicts this early concept for the Balrog wreathed
in flame and roaring. It was quickly apparent to Weta's
designers that the Balrog would pose a very tricky design
challenge. More important than issues of anatomy and form
became the issues of light and dark, shadow and flame,
which essentially is what the Balrog is.

▶ **THE BALROG**
Concept sketches
John Howe
"The Balrog was fun to think about because of all the creatures, it's the one
that divides the fans. Tolkien was always a little brief in his description, so
people interpret it in different ways. I mean, I've always drawn him with
wings because it just seems so cool to have wings! There's a hint of it in the
book when Tolkien says, 'There are shadows, like wings', and frankly that
was all the excuse I needed to stick wings on it. It doesn't say they don't
have wings, so why not? That was Peter's tongue-in-cheek approach, too! If
it doesn't say it's not there — then we can do it!"

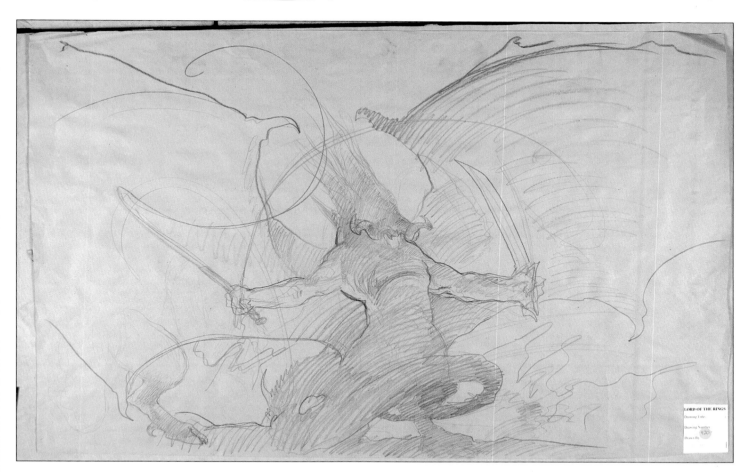

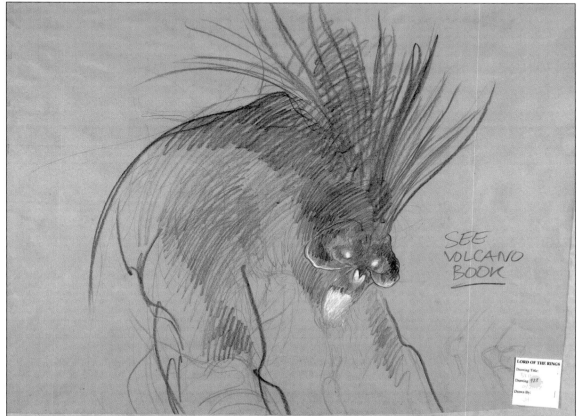

SEE
VOLCANO
BOOK

THE BALROG
Concept maquettes
Jamie Beswarick &
Ben Wootten
To the right is an early design for the Balrog's head by Jamie. Opposite and overleaf is the final approved design maquette by Ben, with colour scheme by Gino Acevedo. Various photographs were made of the maquette, exploring how it would appear from all angles. Similarly, once painted, the sculpture was photographed under different lighting conditions to explore how it might be treated with different effects.

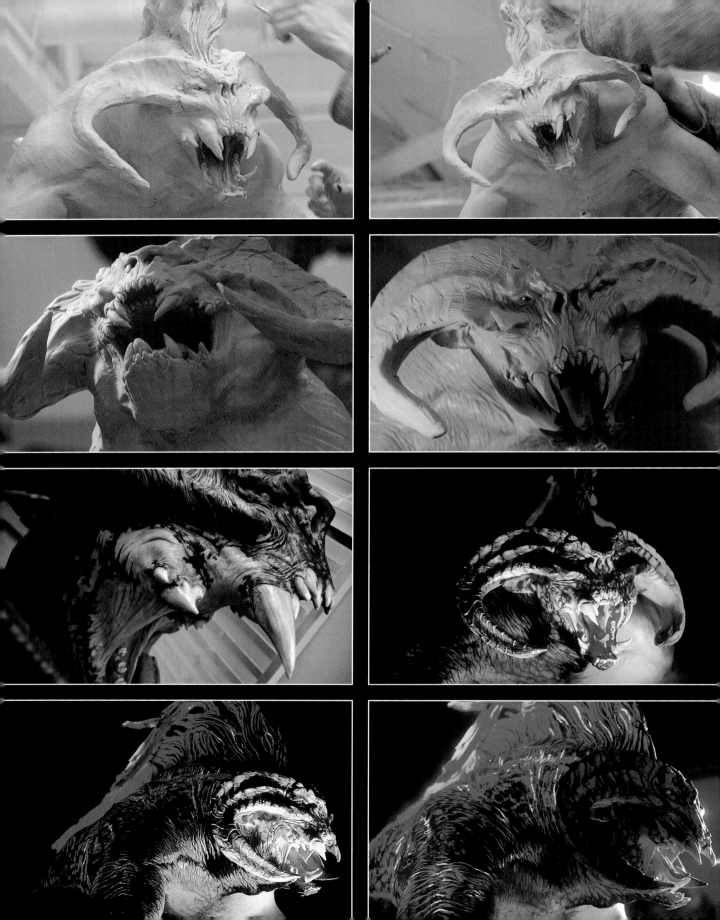

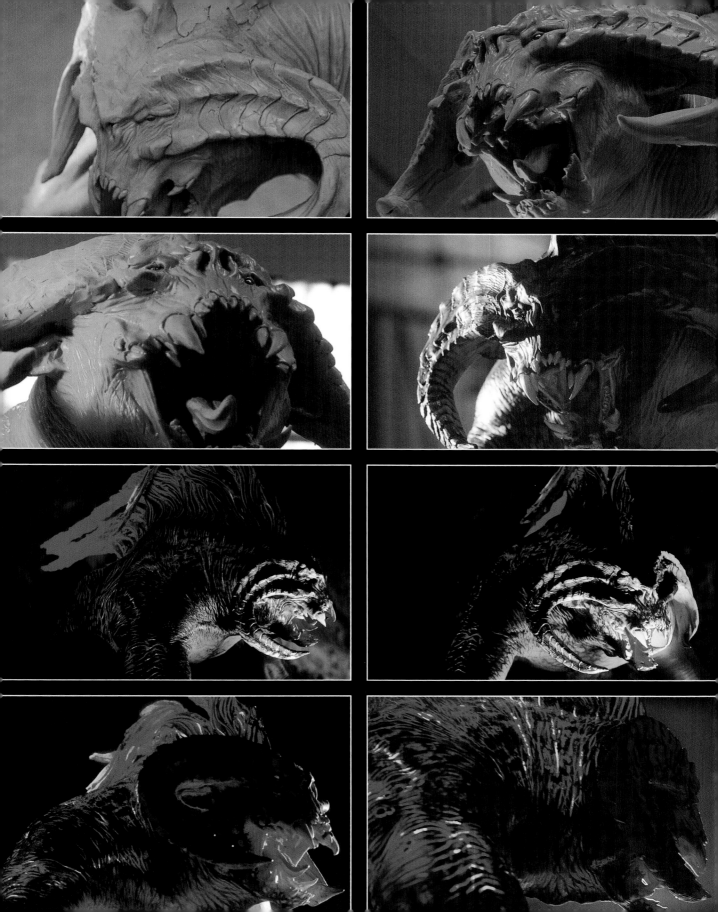

Credits

THE LORD OF THE RINGS
THE FELLOWSHIP OF THE RING

Conceptual Designers
Alan Lee
John Howe

Production Designer
Grant Major

Costume Designer
Ngila Dickson

Director of Miniatures Photography
Alex Funke

WETA WORKSHOP LTD
Creature, Miniature, Armour, Weapons, Special Make-up Effects Supervisor
Richard Taylor

Designers/Sculptors
Jamie Beswarick
Shaun Bolton
Daniel Falconer
Warren Mahy
Ben Wootten
Sacha Lees
Johnny Brough
Sourisak Chanpaseuth
Bill Hunt

Prosthetics Supervisor
Gino Acevedo

Senior Miniature Technicians
Paul Van Ommen
John Baster
Mary MacLachlan

Photoshop Artist
Mel James

VISUAL EFFECTS ART DEPARTMENT
Visual Effects Art Directors
Paul Lasaine
Jeremy Bennett

Photoshop Artist
Gus Hunter

3D Previs Artist
Imery Watson

WETA DIGITAL LTD
Visual Effects Art Director
Christian Rivers

Matt Painters
Max Dennison
Wayne Haag
Yanick Dusseault
Roger Kupelian
Laurent Ben-Mimoun

To be continued in…

The Art of

THE TWO TOWERS
THE LORD OF THE RINGS™